12-28-76

CHRISTIANS AND MARXISTS

CHRISTIANS AND MARXISTS

The Mutual Challenge to Revolution

by

José Míguez-Bonino

first delivered as
The 1974 London Lecture
in Contemporary Christianity
(Chairman: John Stott)

WILLIAM B. EERDMANS PUBLISHING COMPANY
GRAND RAPIDS, MICHIGAN

To my sons Néstor and Eduardo,
in the long conversations with
whom I have learned more than
in many books.

1944905

The London Lectures in Contemporary Christianity, in-
augurated in 1974, are designed to stimulate Christian
thinking on some of the burning issues of the day. The
sponsoring body is the Langham Trust. Any enquiries should
be addressed to the Trustees, 2, All Souls Place, London W1.

PREFACE

THE CHRISTIAN/MARXIST discussion (criticism, apologetics, dialogue) already has a long history in Europe. To review critically the literature that it has produced would in itself be a major task, which I am neither competent nor inclined to undertake. My only justification for daring to accept the invitation to deliver the *London Lectures in Contemporary Christianity* on this subject and to publish the text lies in the fact that, being a Latin American and having participated in the life of the churches and society in a modest way for thirty years, I can hope to bring to this discussion certain particular perspectives and insights which are the result of the Latin American experience.

Perhaps it is just as well that I state explicitly from the very beginning the presuppositions from which this book is written. Some readers may thus be spared the effort of reading further. Others may be helped to put what they read in perspective.

This book is written from the point of view of a person who confesses Jesus Christ as his Lord and Saviour. This is his centre of gravity and everything else is seen (in intention, at least) in relation to it. The reality and power of the Triune God, the witness of Holy Scriptures, the story of God's salvation are not seen as hypotheses to be proved, but as the foundation of life, action, understanding and hope. This presupposition belongs, to be sure, to the realm of faith and therefore can only be justified eschatologically, when faith becomes sight, 'and all men shall see him'.

A second presupposition belongs to the level of history: as a Latin American Christian I am convinced — with many other Latin Americans who have tried to understand the situation of

7

our people and to place it in world perspective—that revolutionary action aimed at changing the basic economic, political, social and cultural structures and conditions of life is imperative today in the world. Ours is not a time for mere development, rearranging or correction, but for basic and revolutionary change (which ought not to be equated necessarily with violence). The possibility for human life to remain human on our planet hangs on our ability to effect this change. Such a conviction can only partially be justified in discussion: convictions in the area of history can be theoretically explained but they can only be proved *practically*—by turning them into history.

Still in another level lies the presupposition—which I shall try to argue throughout the book—that the socioanalytical tools, the historical horizon of interpretation, the insight into the dynamics of the social process and the revolutionary ethos and programme which Marxism has either received and appropriated or itself created are, however corrected or reinterpreted, indispensable for revolutionary change.

To bring together these vastly different presuppositions is the task to which I shall try to make a very small contribution. Our total experience as Latin American Christians convinces us that it is possible, and indeed necessary, to establish these correlations. But it also convinces us that this will not happen mainly through theoretical discussion—and least of all through syncretic or compromising arrangements—but in actual historical engagement. Reflection must be placed at the service of such action, but it cannot be dispensed with nor its importance minimised. It must accompany the experience of success and failure, it must try to penetrate the nature of our practical dilemmas, frustrations and drawbacks in order to overcome them and it must temper and give consistence to our enthusiasm.

On the basis of this approach, we cannot leave aside some important theoretical questions concerning Marxism. This is the reason why I have been forced to take up and even to make options in relation to some complex socioanalytical and philosophical questions on which I can claim no particular expertise. Thus, the theoretical discussion in chapters five and six, while perhaps boring to Christians who have no particular interest in internal Marxist discussion and inadequate to Marxists who have a deep knowledge of them, seems to me a necessary step in the argument. The same thing must be said, *mutatis mutandis*, of the theological discussion in chapters two, four and seven. The discussion of the criticism of religion (chapters three and four) corresponds to a more classical aspect of the dialogue, but I have tried to put it in the perspective of the Latin American experience which is presented in the first chapter. The last two chapters are an attempt to draw some ethical/practical consequences from the total argument.

The whole book is, in a way, a series of 'soundings'. Hence the incomplete and truncated character of some of our discussions, both in relation to the Marxist sources and development and to the total theological and Biblical material. In many cases I have included references for the interested reader to pursue. Thus, the nature of this work is that of an invitation to conversation and study rather than that of a developed and finished thesis.

The magnitude of my indebtedness precludes the attempt to mention names. Beyond the many friends with whom we have often pondered these themes is the 'cloud of witnesses', the many who in my continent and around the world have found in their generous and unrestricted engagement in the struggle of the poor for the transformation of this world a way of responding to the challenge and of expressing their gratitude to the grace which they have found in the Crucified and Risen One, the one New Man in whose image lies the hope and the future of mankind. I cannot, nevertheless, silence my deep recognition and gratitude to the sponsors of the London Lectures, and particularly to the chairman of the Board, the Reverend John Stott, whose friendship is the best reward for the small effort and the unjustified daring of accepting this task. I have not found in him or the other evangelical friends who have sponsored these lectures either dogmatic critics or accommodating flatterers but a group of deeply committed Christians seriously trying to come to grips, in the life of society, with the implications of their faith. The frank and enlightening conversations which usually followed the lectures have made a great difference at many points between the oral version and this book. Of course, I am the only one responsible for the positions and points of view expressed. But these friends will frequently find their concerns and observations taken up in the discussion. I must also recognise my debt to my friends and colleagues Lee Brummel and Sidney Rooy for their courageous attempt to create some sense and readability out of my barbarous English; if at some points they have failed, the reader may imagine what the original was like!

This author is neither a politician nor a sociologist. He is a theologian trying to discharge his political responsibility as theologian, which means at the theoretical level that corresponds to academic work, with all its dangers and frustrations. But, to the extent that the position taken in this book is correct, such work can only have meaning if it faithfully assumes, in the light of the Gospel, the real commitment of Christians and offers a possibility of deepening, correcting and strengthening such commitment.

JOSÉ MÍGUEZ BONINO

Buenos Aires, Advent 1974.

TABLE OF CONTENTS

CONTENTS

CHAPTER I

COMMUNISTS AND
THEOLOGIANS

FIDEL CASTRO IS reported to have said, half-jokingly, that he felt rather confused because 'theologians are becoming communists and communists are becoming theologians'. This remark belongs in the context of a number of long and sometimes elaborate discussions in which the Cuban premier referred (particularly during his visit to Chile, Peru and Ecuador in 1971) to 'the recent fact' of 'a growing number of priests and Christians in general who have a definite participation in the process of liberation'.[1] There will be occasion to return at a later point to some of Castro's observations; at present it is necessary only to point out that the magnitude of the movement to which he alludes is such that no revolutionary Marxist in Latin America can afford to ignore it. Juan Rosales, an Argentine Marxist author who has given careful attention — and much incisive criticism — to the role of religion in our society, makes this rather startling assertion:

> ... the bringing about of a true revolutionary transformation in our country ... is for us (communists) *inconceivable* without the resolute participation of a renewed and engaged Christianity, which is equipped to make its specific contribution to the revolutionary baggage.[2]

Co-operation rather than dialogue

The fact is there. Interpretations and reactions are multiple

15

and contradictory. But right and left, ecclesiastical hierarchies and the common man in the street, the social analyst and the journalist, Latin Americans and foreign observers are equally arrested by this new phenomenon: not a Christian–Marxist dialogue but a growing and overt common participation in a revolutionary project, the basic lines of which are undoubtedly based on a Marxist analysis.

Two characteristics of this relation should be immediately underlined. The first is that the relationship is quite lucid and conscious — at least among the leading participants. The Puerto Rican professor of theology Luis N. Rivera quotes with approval the remark of the Italian Waldensian Mario Miegge: 'I *confess* that I am a Christian, but I *declare* myself a Marxist.' This position, adds Rivera, represents that of many Latin American Christians 'who find in Marxism a language of liberation adequate to articulate their revolutionary intention'.[3] The communist Rosales is right when he says that, just as it is inconceivable for a revolutionary in Latin America to forego the participation of committed Christians, 'it should be inconceivable for progressive Christians' to envisage a revolution 'without the orientating contribution of Marxism-Leninism or without the protagonistic activity of the working class'.[4]

A second characteristic of the Marxist/Christian relationship is also implicit in these quotations: they all refer to a common revolutionary project. The well-known French Marxist Roger Garaudy has said that 'dialogue is not an end in itself: it issues in concrete co-operation in order to respond to the crucial problems of our time: war and social revolution'.[5] But in Latin America the order seems to be reversed: co-operation leads to dialogue. This is so because, as J. de Santa Ana argues, 'the circumstances that condition the situation of individuals, not communist ideology, constitute the true challenge for the Church'.[6] In other words, it is not an intellectual dialogue that leads to co-operation; rather the objective conditions prompt a common action, and it is within this co-operation that dialogue takes place. The Dominican Lawrence Bright has correctly understood the situation when he writes:

To be a Christian and a Marxist is normal enough in, for example, South America where the culture is Catholic but the social situation is sufficiently bad to make revolution an obvious necessity. When one is dispossessed one is not a revolutionary simply on principle; what has to be done is clear, and one sets about doing it without waiting for justification from the Christian gospel or Marxist philosophy. One is Christian and Marxist because that's how things are.[7]

These quotations raise still another point. Rivera speaks of Marxism as 'a language of liberation' which is useful 'for the articulation of a revolutionary intention'. De Santa Ana and Bright relate 'communist ideology' or 'Marxist philosophy' to liberation or revolution. When asked whether a Christian had to become a Marxist in order to make Christian love effective in social practice, Fidel Castro answered: 'Nobody can love all men and be anti-Marxist *in the social meaning of the term* . . . To be Christian and Marxist in economy, in politics and in all these things, without entering the field of philosophy, which is never debated among us.'[8] Is this possible? Can Marxism be understood merely as a form of social analysis or as a political programme? And how is Christianity to function in this perspective: only as a motivating force or ethical justification? Does it have any social and political contents of its own? Some of these questions are being raised more and more sharply in our discussions in Latin America and will occupy our attention in later chapters. At this point, we shall try to follow more carefully the movement through which Christians and Marxists have arrived at this strange relationship.

A Christian pilgrimage to Marxism?

It is not my intention to restrict our consideration to the Latin American perspective. But it still seems profitable to dwell on it in so far as it helps to pose some of the relevant problems in a fruitful perspective, both from a Christian and a Marxist point of view, namely, that of concrete historical facts and situations. In fact, my basic contention throughout this book will be that the theoretical considerations or the theological arguments that we

17

shall entertain are meaningful only because, and in so far as, they are demanded by a Christian's active obedience and are able to correct, deepen and make this obedience more fruitful. As Hugo Assmann puts it:

> Perhaps one of the deepest coincidences between a non-dogmatic Marxism and an authentically Biblical Christianity lies precisely in this, that both have an absolutely peculiar relation to truth. Both of them demand that their truth be 'verified', that it 'become true', that it be fulfilled. They demand to be confirmed by the facts. They conceive of truth as truth in the facts and it is precisely in this that they stand opposed to all forms of idealism, metaphysics or ideology that understand truth as something 'in itself', outside the facts, in a 'separate realm'.[9]

Such a Christian/Marxist relationship cannot be taken for granted. The observer is bound to ask how is it possible that a significant number of Christians—who as a whole ten years ago were militantly anti-communist and thought of their faith as a retaining wall or as an alternative against the progress of Marxism —have come to declare themselves Marxists, even in this restricted sense of the word? How is it possible that Marxists— who even into the sixties in Latin America were militantly anti-clerical and repeated with fervour all the traditional slogans against religion—have come to see Christians as 'strategic allies', as indispensable partners in revolution? An adequate answer to these questions would demand a careful historical investigation. It is a long process in which several kinds of factors have been operative. We cannot at present attempt such a research, but it will be necessary to indicate, however briefly, the general path that this pilgrimage has taken. Consequently, drawing in part from personal experience, in part from some research in the development of Christian social thinking and involvement in the last fifteen years, and in part from direct acquaintance with many of the protagonists of this process, I shall dare to submit an approach to what I have called—somewhat provocatively— 'a Christian pilgrimage to Marxism'.

It is my thesis that, as Christians, confronted by the inhuman conditions of existence prevailing in the continent, they have tried to make their Christian faith historically relevant, they have been increasingly compelled to seek an analysis and historical programme for their Christian obedience. At this point, the dynamics of the historical process, both in its objective conditions and its theoretical development, have led them, through the failure of several remedial and reformist alternatives, to discover the unsubstitutable relevance of Marxism.

This complicated and involved formulation tries to synthesise a process that we shall now try to clarify and illustrate.[10] Firstly, a few comments for clarification: (1) The pioneers in this development have been mostly clergymen, university students or professionals; they belong sociologically to the *petite* bourgeoisie rather than to the working classes; their concern for revolutionary change was not so much the result of a direct experience of destitution and poverty as of the combination of a sense of solidarity with the oppressed and a theoretical insight into the social conditions prevailing in the continent. (2) The road is marked for many of these Christians by an experience of the social irrelevance of traditional charity and liberal reformism. This irrelevance was felt among Christians both as individuals and as organised groups (ecclesiastical social action, participation in Christian co-operatives, Christian trade unions, student groups or parties): a structural-political approach was the only option left. (3) The failure of Christian Democratic parties — particularly in Chile — convinced these Christians that 'third ways' between capitalism and socialism involving purely idealistic and voluntaristic approaches to structural change were inadequate and ill-fated. The decision for Marxism is therefore an option for structural over against purely individual change, for revolution over against reformism, for socialism over against capitalist development or 'third' solutions, for 'scientific' over against idealistic or utopian socialism. (4) The fact that these Christians were not looking primarily for a theoretical answer to philosophical or existential problems but rather for a relevant way to make their action historically efficacious, results in a great freedom in relation to the total Marxist philosophy, in a rejection of all

dogmatism both in theoretical formulation and political programme, in an openness and eagerness to accept new questions
and to develop new solutions.

We can now illustrate some of these points by means of two
examples. On the one hand, we shall follow the argument
developed by one of the pioneers of a new Christian revolutionary
consciousness in Latin America, Camilo Torres. On the other,
we shall look briefly into the development of Catholic political
forces in Chile. Many more illustrations could be produced. An
exhaustive study of this process should follow systematically
these developments in a larger historical and geographical scope.
But I think these instances will prove representative.

Camilo Torres has come to represent for Latin American
Christians the best example of 'conversion' to a Marxist-oriented
revolutionary theory and practice: as an example to be followed
or rejected. He is often presented as an enthusiastic, almost a
fanatic. But his decisions – whether right or wrong – are usually
carefully reasoned and supported by a cogent argument. His
lecture, 'Revolution: Christian imperative', presented in Louvain
(Belgium) in September 1964, one year before he enrolled in the
guerrilla, eighteen months before his death, is an excellent
summary of his view.[11] The carefully constructed argument –
almost scholastic in its rigorous logic – moves along three main
stages. The first one is theological: the essential mission of the
Church is spreading the new life in Christ, which has a divine
origin and becomes manifest in efficacious love for one's neighbour. In a situation in which poverty is rampant, such a love
must necessarily become active in assisting men who suffer from
poverty. The second stage of the argument marks the transition
to the structural dimension. He asks under which conditions it
would be possible, in the situation obtaining in the Third World,
most effectively to plan for economic development which could
cope with the problems of poverty. He then considers the
characteristics of capitalist and socialist planning, as well as the
peculiar conditions and obstacles in the underdeveloped countries.
The conclusions reached are that effective development can best
be achieved within a socialist context and that this will not take
place unless strong pressure for change develops from the lower

strata of society. Revolutionary change can be either violent or peaceful according to the relative interaction between pressure from below and resistance or flexibility for change from above. Then, we move through a second transition to a third stage in the argument: how can Christians best contribute to this kind of planning through which their active love can become historically significant? It might be ideally desirable that Christians would undertake the leadership of this task. But it is clear that, on the whole, they do not have the competence, and indeed not even the will and purpose to do it, while Marxists – whatever their shortcomings (to which Camilo is by no means blind!) – have a social understanding, a political discipline and an ideological perspective which have proved to be effective. On the other hand, there are the drawbacks of Marxist dogmatism and some of their methods. This is the final conclusion:

> To seek authoritative economic planning in the poor countries is generally an obligation for the Christian. This planning is essential to efficacy in the authentic service of the majorities and therefore it is a condition of charity in these countries . . . It is most probable that the Marxists will take over the leadership of this planning. In this case, the Christian must collaborate insofar as his moral principles will permit, keeping in mind the obligation of avoiding greater evils and of seeking the common good.[12]

Let us now look at a corporate development: the participation in politics of Catholic Christians in Chile, the place in which the support of a significant, organised and articulate number of Christians for a Marxist-led programme (the FRAP of Salvador Allende) reached its most important expression. Until the 1880s the Conservative Party had represented the interests of the rich landowners and the political concerns of the Roman Catholic Church in Chile – basically restricted to the struggle against secularisation and liberalism, the preservation of the 'rights' of the Church in education, marriage legislation and other aspects of the national life, and certain forms of public morals. When the trade union movement began, in the second half of the last century, the Church limited itself to denouncing it at first and then to forming 'Catholic workers' unions' in order to 'protect' the Catholic workers from 'foreign ideologies'. When the workers' movement gathered strength and conflicts became more radical during the first decades of this century, it became clear that Christians could not continue to act simply as a dyke against it. Papal encyclicals authorised the search for more positive responses. Groups of Catholics moved in Chile from the stage of 'contention against socialism' to that of 'a Christian alternative' to it. This phase covers at least three attempts: (1) To promote, within the Conservative Party, a pressure group which, inspired by the co-operative ideas originating in Europe, tries to offer a Christian way between capitalism and socialism, retaining private ownership of the means of production but organising certain forms of corporate ownership and political participation; (2) When the fascist face of corporativism makes it unacceptable, this group tries to define more clearly its options in terms of co-participation of the workers, the co-operation of social classes and certain forms of land-reform and the repossession of the resources of the country dominated by foreign concerns: at this point they are forced to break away from the Conservative Party and to form their own political party, 'La Falange Nacional' (1939); (3) It became then necessary to find an ideology, an analysis of the situation and a political project: the *Falange* becomes the seed of a party, the Christian Democratic Party.

The philosophy of the new party is the 'Christian Humanism' of Jacques Maritain. The social analysis and the political programme are elaborated with the help of European intellectuals of the Christian Democratic parties. The party calls for 'a revolution in freedom', within the constitutional order, following 'a Christian solution' opposed both to the liberal-capitalist and to the Marxist-communist programme. Specifically, it advocated co-operation over against the struggle of social classes, a mixed economy over against the socialisation of the means of production, an advantageous arrangement with foreign owners of copper and other basic resources instead of nationalisation. It also promised a number of social reforms: land reform, education, housing and other social benefits. On this programme, the Christian Democratic Party came to power in 1964. Three years later, the more progressive sector of it broke away and formed a new party — the MAPU. The reason: the failure of the party, now in power, to carry out its programme. None of the major reforms that had been promised could be realised: the local economic oligarchy and foreign concerns retained their stranglehold on the economy, the key landholdings had not been touched, social conflicts had increased. The Christian Democratic government, far from being an alternative to both capitalism and communism, was only a means of preserving the capitalist system. Christianity had merely been used to prevent a real revolution. The MAPU became, in the next election, part of the socialist-communist coalition. Since then, and up to the military coup that interrupted the constitutional order and 'the Chilean road to socialism', at least two more groups have broken away from the Christian Democratic Party, rejected the idea of 'a third way', 'a Christian alternative', and entered the socialist camp. The process leading to these successive fractions is well described by a leader of the latest one, 'Izquierda Cristiana', Dr. Bosco Parra:

Our socialist conviction is the product of our reformist experience. Capitalism, modernised with some elements of agrarian reform, proved unable to obtain growth. At the same time, we came to understand that a socialist perspective cannot be built except in the complete social and political unity of the working people.[13]

Christians: the strategic allies

Before turning to some of the theological questions pertinent to the evaluation of Christian-Marxist co-operation, we must look back at this 'strategic alliance' and ask how have the Marxists arrived at the attitude reflected in Fidel Castro's now famous expression. I will now submit a second part of the hypothesis explored in the preceding pages. In relation to the development among Marxists, it would run like this:

The Latin American revolutionary is confronted with a state of consciousness in the masses (particularly but not exclusively in the rural population) *in which the slave relationship of traditional society, the cultural alienation imposed by imperialism and the magical forms of folk-religion have produced a lag in the revolutionary consciousness in relation to the demands of the objective situation. In the effort to change this situation, the Marxist revolutionary has found himself side by side with a number of active revolutionary Christians and has discovered, in the new movement within the Christian fold, the potential motivating and mobilising power of the Christian faith for revolutionary change.*

I have cast this affirmation in basically Marxist categories, partly because they accurately portray the situation but also because we are trying to establish the way in which a revolutionary Marxist arrives at this attitude. It is important to note at the outset that such a change in the attitude of a number of Marxists is not the result of a theoretical elaboration, but has been made possible by the *fact* of the existence of revolutionary Christians. It must also be noticed that the problem of revolutionary consciousness is not an abstract question but one which grows out of revolutionary action itself and is, therefore, for a Marxist, an eminently legitimate problem, whatever the correct answer may be.

I shall now try to explain and comment on this interpretation.

(1) It is well known that a revolutionary situation is for Marxism the result of the combination of objective and subjective factors. The objective conditions are well defined in a famous paragraph of Marx's prologue to his 'Contribution to the Critique of Political Economy',[14] and can be summarised for our purposes by saying that they occur when the 'relations of production' obtaining in a society (the ways in which society is organised for production—for instance, the forms of property and labour) are no longer able to facilitate the expansion of the forces of production (man's effort to produce the material elements for his life) but rather block this growth. Man experiences this contradiction in different forms: either directly as need or in a sublimated (and disguised) form as subjective unhappiness, religious aspiration or moral dissatisfaction. Revolutionary consciousness is born when man (specifically the proletariat in the present situation)

sees (even in a partially ideological way) that this unhappiness has its basis in the present organisation of the process of production. He therefore consciously takes up his historical task of changing it. Such a consciousness cannot emerge, to be sure, except on the basis of objective contradiction. Marx uses strong analogies such as 'reflection' or 'echo' to indicate the dependence of subjective consciousness on objective conditions. But many careful studies have shown that he does not see human consciousness as a mere reflection or a mechanic consequence: the influence of the past, and ideological and religious mystification, can block the awareness of real objective conditions. Positively, therefore, there is also the pedagogical task of overcoming this lag and of awakening consciousness.

(2) The history of Marxist parties and movements in Latin America has been particularly pathetic in relation to this pedagogical task. Although we will not enter here into such a history, it can be summarised in Sotelo's conclusion[15] that, wherever there has been a well-structured Marxist party with a clear revolutionary theory, it has failed to make an impact on the masses and therefore it has remained an isolated elite—and, wherever there have been popular movements with a wide basis, they have been populist movements, lacking a clear theoretical analysis and a revolutionary theory. There are, to be sure, exceptions to this generalisation (Chile, and Uruguay to a certain point), but that it generally applies is enough to suggest the seriousness of the situation. Guevara's diary of his tragic campaign in Bolivia bears out the painful revolutionary frustration: it reiterates month after month that 'the peasant basis remains undeveloped'; peasants are afraid, distrustful, they cling to their ways, they inform the army, at most they trade with the guerrillas —but there is no revolutionary spark, there are only 'the empty faces'.[16]

(3) There are, undoubtedly, a number of factors involved in this situation. But among them, religion plays a significant role at least in two ways—to which we shall return in the third chapter. In the first place, popular or folk religion acts as an integrating force for the tendencies and relations of traditional society: it gives them religious sanction, it expresses in mythical

ways the relations of dependence, it reinforces a passive attitude. It is not an atheist critic but a Roman Catholic meeting of catechists that reaches this devastating conclusion:

> The manifestations of popular religion—although they sometimes have positive aspects—are, in relation to the rapid evolution of society, the expression of alienated groups, namely, groups which live in a depersonalised, conformist and uncritical way and make no effort to change society. This sort of religiosity is maintained and partly stimulated by the dominant structures, to which the Church belongs ... The expansion of this type of religion delays in its turn the necessary change in the structures of society.[17]

The quotation points already to a second aspect, not only is traditional folk religion in itself such a blocking element: there is also a constant ideological manipulation of religious motivations, slogans, traditions, in order to buttress the *status quo*. Hugo Assmann speaks in this respect of 'an ideological surplus value' of the Christian faith which is constantly appropriated by the reactionaries,[18] or of 'the religious spare parts' which bourgeois ideology is always ready to use.[19]

(4) These facts demand recognition. Perhaps the failure of much revolutionary propaganda can be traced to a large extent to the inability to deal seriously with this fundamental fact: the depth to which Christianity—as a sociological entity—has penetrated and still moulds the Latin American consciousness at a visceral level where theoretical, rational explanation fails to make an impact ... even when it has an objective basis. People 'live' their economic and social alienation in a world of mythical representation which political ideology is not able to pierce.[20] It is in the face of this situation that Marxists have become startled at first, then interested and even attracted by the emergence of persons and groups which seem to be able to break the spell of this alienation *from within the religious consciousness itself*. This movement within Christianity is particularly interesting for active revolutionaries like Castro or Guevara who are more concerned about revolutionary action than theoretical explana-

tion. But we have seen that even a dogmatic orthodox communist like Rosales cannot fail to take it into account. There are already some studies exploring the psychological and sociological structures at work both in the religious 'blocking' of a revolutionary attitude and in the 'religious un-blocking' which takes place in these recent movements.[21] Hugo Assmann advances the hypothesis that:

> ... the imposed and internalised oppressive context in which the oppressed consciousness is found must be also the starting point for its liberation, which must proceed through a necessary revolutionary implementation of 'their Christianity'.[22]

This is the context in which, as Assmann himself points out, we must read pronouncements such as those we have quoted before, or the famous paragraph of Guevara:

> Christians must definitively decide for revolution, particularly in our continent, where the Christian faith is so important among the masses of the people . . . When Christians will dare to give a total revolutionary testimony the Latin American revolution will be invincible, because until now Christians have allowed their doctrine to be instrumentalised by reactionaries.[23]

(5) Expressions like those we have just quoted, and the programme implicit in them, raise a number of questions. On the practical level, the presence of 'strategic allies' particularly active in political conscientisation and the organisation of the people while maintaining an open Christian witness, creates for Marxists an important problem: the need to soft-pedal, if not to withdraw altogether, the insistence on the absolute character of a dialectical materialism which has played a prominent part in the strategy of the Communist parties, and which demanded an all-out war on religion in any form. We know how adamant Lenin was on this question.[24] If Christians themselves are entrusted with the struggle against the paralysing and reactionary manipulation of religion, the perspective from which they will act is bound to be

different from the classic Marxist approach. If the revolution is 'the art of adding up', as Castro has said, a certain doctrinal latitude is inevitable on the part of Marxists. Philosophical and ideological aspects will have to be relegated to one side to make way for the more immediate political, economic and social questions. Any Marxist who knows the history of his movement cannot fail to be concerned with the danger of falling prey to 'opportunism'.

But there are also questions for the Christian. On the one hand, it becomes imperative to understand the historical and theological significance of this 'instrumentalisation' of the Christian faith to which Guevara referred and to judge it from the point of view of the Biblical faith itself. To this we shall turn in the third chapter. But it is also necessary to ask whether revolutionary Christians are in turn 'instrumentalising' the Christian faith in a different direction. Is it legitimate from a Biblical point of view to locate the field of action of the Christian faith at the historical level of social and political life? This emphasis can by no means be taken for granted as the most authentic expression of the Christian faith in view of a long and significant tradition in the churches that has restricted Christianity to the level of the 'inner' or 'spiritual' life and of individual ethics. To this question we turn our attention in the next chapter.

CHAPTER II

BLESSED ARE THE DOERS

THE NATURE OF the encounter and relationship between Christians and Marxists that we have described as characteristic of the Latin American situation has certain parallels with events in other parts of the world, particularly in Europe. In the two cases, mutual anathema has given place—as the Marxist Garaudy has said—to dialogue. In both cases, the dialogue is seen in the context of the search of mankind for a better form of life, for a more just and human society. Both contemplate, therefore, the possibility of dialogue issuing—as Garaudy has said in a sentence quoted before—in co-operation. But there is, together with these similarities, a striking difference between the two approaches. The European 'dialogue' frequently begins with the existence of two 'systems of truth', two self-contained and self-sufficient conceptual entities, almost two ideologies which confront each other, compare their views and derive from them certain practical conclusions on the basis of which co-operation is either possible or excluded. In the Latin American situation, on the other hand, we are faced with men who are engaged in certain forms of action in relation to given conditions. These courses of action are, to be sure, related to theoretical views and horizons of meaning. But it is not as conceptual vision but as historical practice that they come into contact, opposition or co-operation. Consequently, the theoretical discussion—the 'dialogue' in the European sense of the word—arises as the explication, background and projection of this practice.

We must not exaggerate this difference. But it is important

to notice it because it raises a crucial theological question: the relation of truth to practice or, in theological terms, of knowledge to obedience. The classical approach, which is deeply embedded in the theological tradition, conceives truth as the correspondence between certain conceptual formulations and universal ideas or principles. The realm of action corresponds, therefore, to a second level: that of the 'consequences' or 'inferences' of these truths. This distinction, which is clearly rooted in a form of idealistic philosophy, has some momentous consequences for our subject. On the one hand, it makes possible a discussion between ideas, or theories, without taking into account the historical courses of action to which such ideas are related, i.e. the debate between a Marxism which is not related to the actual history of the socialist movements, the trade unions, the socialist countries and a Christianity which is exempted from giving account for its historical embodiments in the Middle Ages, or during the Industrial Revolution, or in the conquest and colonisation of the Americas. Secondly, it sees ideas as floating in a heaven of abstraction, as if they were born out of nothing, unrelated to the conditions of existence of the peoples and groups in which they were conceived. Thirdly, this conception creates all the classical ethical dilemmas by positing an 'ideal course of action', derived from the conceptual firmament of truth and asking afterwards for the degree of 'compromise' permissible to accommodate the actual conditions in which action has to be undertaken.

The inadequacy of the idealistic perspective has been clearly exposed both from a philosophical and from a psycho-sociological point of view. The recognition that our ideas, our personal and social behaviour and the conditions in which we live continually interact in a totality which can only be distinguished for theoretical purposes but not separated, is by no means a peculiar view of Marxists, although they have elaborated a particular understanding of this fact. But I am concerned now with the question whether this idealistic perspective, which has dominated so much the theological scene, corresponds to the Biblical understanding of truth and knowledge. Or is Assmann justified when he claims, rejecting this conception, that truth is for the Bible 'truth in the facts'? The question is by no means insignificant because it affects our whole understanding of Christian commitment. Much Biblical research in the last decades is relevant to our question. It is not possible now to enter with any detail into this material. But we must look, however briefly and incompletely, to some specific Biblical texts. Although neither the competence of the author nor the nature of this book correspond to the area of exegesis, we cannot evade the need to look carefully to particular Biblical passages because we have no other source of final knowledge of God than his own self-identification in Jesus Christ. And this knowledge is not available for us except in the witness of the Old and New Testament. The Biblical record is a text and must be approached as such, that is, taking pains to understand its meaning through careful and detailed exegesis. If a literalist interpretation has many times forced the text in order to accommodate preconceived theological formulae, modern liberal interpretation has done no better: the presuppositions and dogmas of idealistic philosophy, the ethical principles of rationalism and the values of the modern bourgeois world have determined what the Bible could or could not say — or what should and should not be taken seriously. The arbitrariness of such a procedure is clearly illustrated in the question we face now: the nature of knowledge and truth according to the Bible and the relation of the knowledge of God to inter-human relationships.

The knowledge of God

In the impossibility of presenting a complete Biblical study of our theme, I shall confine myself to some instances from two blocks of Biblical material which are particularly relevant: the prophetic and the Johannine understanding of 'the knowledge of God'.[1]

'The knowledge of the Lord' or 'to know the Lord' is, for prophetic literature, a very important expression. It summarises what is demanded from Israel; it is the condition made possible by the covenant and it is the promise and hope for renewal and perfection in the 'new covenant'. We can begin our exploration with a classical text from the twenty-second chapter of the book of Jeremiah:

13 Woe to him who builds his house by unrighteousness,
and his upper rooms by injustice;
who makes his neighbour serve him for nothing,
and does not give him his wages;

14 who says, 'I will build myself a great house
with spacious upper rooms',
and cuts out windows for it,
panelling it with cedar,
and painting it with vermilion.

15 Do you think you are a king because you compete in cedar?
Did not your father eat and drink and *do justice and
righteousness?*
Then it was all well with him.

16 *He judged the cause of the poor and the needy;*
Then it was well.
Is not this to know me?
Says the Lord.

The prophet is comparing the reign of Jehoiakim with that of
his father Josiah. The expressions used to praise the latter
(verse 15) are a well-known formula which defines the function
of government in Israel. In contrast, Jehoiakim follows the
usages and characteristics of the absolute kings of the neighbour-
ing countries (verses 14, 15a). Then, interestingly enough, the
contrast becomes an opposition between 'knowing' and 'not
knowing' the Lord. And, in a striking sentence, the prophet asks:
'Is not this [i.e. Josiah's way of conducting himself as king]
to know me?' Surprised exegetes usually comment that these
actions are 'the consequence of', or 'a sign of' knowing God.
The text simply confronts us with the bold question: 'is not this
to know me?'. In a careful and detailed study of 'knowing God'
in Old Testament usage, G. Johannes Botterweck (who himself
uses the word 'sign' in this connection) cannot avoid the conclusion with regards to this text: 'Fraternal justice is for the king
the *sum total* [or "the essence", *Inbegriff*] of the knowledge of
God'.[2]

32

Another text from the prophet puts this surprising equation in focus:

> Thus says the Lord, 'Let not the wise man glory in his wisdom, let not the mighty man glory in his might, let not the rich man glory in his riches; but let him who glories glory in this, that *he understands and knows me, that I am the Lord who practises steadfast love, justice and righteousness in the earth: for in these things I delight*, says the Lord. (Jeremiah 9:23).

The verse is a brief summary of Jeremiah's understanding of the true relation to the Lord, for the breaking of which Israel has to suffer. Here the basis for the identification between 'knowing God' and 'practising justice' becomes clear: it is Yahweh's own character; he who does not practise justice misunderstands — 'does not know' — God himself. To know the Lord is to pattern one's life after God's own action.

The same theme appears with extraordinary clarity in Hosea, for whom 'the knowledge of the Lord' is a fundamental motif. The references are so frequent and so interwoven that it is impossible to quote them at length. He puts it first in a negative form: 'there is no kindness (*hesed*) or mercy, no *knowledge of God* in the land' (4:1b), explaining immediately: 'there is swearing, lying, stealing' (4:2, a clear reference to the Commandments). A description of the consequent disaster follows, ending with the same motif: 'My people are destroyed for *lack of knowledge*; because you have *rejected knowledge* . . . you have *forgotten the law of your God*' (4:6). In the direct form of commandment the same parallelism appears in chapter six: 'I desire *compassion* and not sacrifice, *knowledge of God* rather than burnt offerings' (6:6b) (a key text for the understanding of the gospel of Matthew, cf. 9:13 and 12:7). The same correlation is found in 10:12, 'Sow for yourselves *righteousness*, reap the fruit of *steadfast love*, for it is time *to seek the Lord*'. This verse, with its expression 'seek the Lord', makes the transition to another related theme: conversion to God. Here again Hosea is very direct: 'So, by the help of your God, *return* (or, "be converted"): *hold fast to love and justice*' (12:6, where there is no justification to correct the text to read, 'return . . . *and* hold fast . . .' as some commentators do). Israel is destroyed for 'lack of knowledge'; the only solution is, therefore, that God himself will again give this knowledge. Hence, as in 12:6, conversion is described as God's own gift. But this does not weaken the ethical connotation of this knowledge. Thus, in 2:19, Yahweh offers 'righteousness, justice, mercy and goodness' as his wedding present to Israel, so that 'you shall know the Lord'.[3] And, in 14:3, when the prophet describes the expected conversion, he contrasts the true God with the false gods whom they have followed: 'We will not again call god the work of our hands, oh Thou *in whom the orphan finds his refuge*.' Here, as in Jeremiah, the juxtaposition of knowledge and justice is grounded in God's own character and action. This is the difference between Yahweh and the idols: to know God is to relate to him in whom the orphan finds protection. As Wolff has summed it up: 'There is no mention, side by side with the ethical area, of a second, heterogeneous, "religious" area, as if the relationship with God were something else side by side with the relationship with the neighbour.'[4]

This is not a peculiarity of Jeremiah and Hosea. Let two other texts suffice to make this point. In the messianic prophecy of Isaiah 11:1–9, the messianic king is announced as the one who will bring forth justice, righteousness and mercy. This will result in the total pacification of creation (cf. the sequence of verses 4–5 and 6 and the same theme in 32:17–18), 'because the earth shall be full of the *knowledge of the Lord*'. In other words, the Lord makes himself known by establishing justice. It is interesting that Habakkuk (2:14) quotes this section of Isaiah (11:9) precisely in this context: God's judgment on those who have built their cities on blood and injustice. God is righteous and will not tolerate oppression and plunder; when he executes his judgment 'the earth will be filled with the *knowledge of the glory of the Lord* as the waters cover the sea'.

Botterweck rightly sums up the result of his study in these words:

In the writings of the pre-exilic prophets as well as in certain sections of the Wisdom literature, the *knowledge of God* means a religious-moral form of conduct of men towards Yahweh: *to know God* means to 'renounce' sin and the worship of idols, to 'return' to Yahweh and to 'seek' for him, to 'depend' upon him and to 'fear' him; it means to 'practise love, justice and righteousness'. He who *knows God* walks in his ways. *Knowledge of God* is active piety.[5]   1944905

This is well said. But it is not enough. It still reflects the 'both-and' formula which we love to use when we don't know how to integrate things which in the Bible are one. The language of the prophets is much bolder: to do justice *is* to know Yahweh. Seen in the perspective of our dichotomising thought, this formulation smacks of an intolerable 'horizontalism'; it seems to be mere humanistic philanthropy, and naturally the interpreters try to supplement it with some 'religious' content. But what needs to be changed is not the Biblical formulation but our perspective. For the Bible, in fact, the practice of justice is not a mere inter-personal relationship or social virtue; it is the very nature of the covenant, because it is a covenant with the Lord who practises justice, with him in whom 'the orphan finds refuge'. Engaging in this course of conduct within the bond of the covenant is to honour Yahweh in the only way in which he can be honoured.

This 'singleness' is most evident in the New Testament literature which has often been considered 'religious' or 'mystical' *par excellence*: the *Johannine Gospel and epistles*. We have now overcome the hermeneutical fashion which treated John as a Hellenising interpretation. More and more Biblical scholars agree that the basic background for these writings must be sought in the Old Testament. The other determining feature of this literature is its uncompromising concentration on the centrality of Jesus Christ. In this sense, John's perspective does not differ from that of the other Gospels: 'these [acts and words of Jesus] are written that you may believe that Jesus is the Christ, the Son of God, and that believing you may have life in his name' (20:31). However different the language, the meaning is the same as that of the other gospels: the Kingdom of God (life) has broken through in Jesus—he is the Christ. Those who stake their future on this fact, enter a new age which, in contrast with the perishing world of darkness and destruction, can be characterised as life, indeed, as 'eternal life'. But how can people who have not heard or seen Jesus partake of this reality? How, to put it in Kierkegaard's terms, can one become contemporary with Christ? John offers two answers, which are summed up in two pregnant verses:

> Truly, truly I say to you, he who *hears my word* and *believes* him who sent me, has eternal life; he does not come into judgment, but *has passed from death to life*. (John 5:24).

> We know that we have *passed out of death into life*, because we *love* the brethren. He *who does not love remains in death*. (John 3:14).

We cannot rest satisfied with a 'both-and' answer, i.e., man needs *both* faith (believing) *and* love. This is not possible because both statements carry a ring of absoluteness; they seem to say, one of them: *nothing but believing* is necessary; and the other, *only love* is necessary. In other words, we seem to find two centres in the Johannine writings: one is christological (1 John 2:23–25; 4:2–3; 5:1–2), and the other ethical (1 John 1:5–7; 2:3–6; 2:8–10; 4:7–8; 4:16) (although I have only taken texts from the epistles, the reader can easily assemble a similar list from the Gospel). How can this apparent contradiction be resolved? Following some observations of J. P. Miranda, I would like to offer the following three points:[6]

(1) John is interested in calling men to become aware of the new situation which has been created within the life of the world through the appearance, ministry, teaching, death and resurrection of Jesus. The messianic Kingdom has arrived, the power of darkness has lost its total sway; the light has come into the world. To believe is to take this news seriously, to acknowledge in Jesus the expected one 'whom the Father has sent' and therefore to take one's place in this radically new situation. There is no possibility of a 'passive' faith in Jesus Christ, because we are not invited to incorporate one more piece of knowledge to our information or to experience a particular form of subjectivity, but to be 'born of God', to 'remain in God', to 'have fellowship

with God', to 'know God', and all these expressions designate a possibility of living a new kind of human life which has *now* (i.e. with the advent of Jesus) become available.

(2) What is this 'new life' which is now possible in the sphere opened by Christ? The Johannine Jesus constantly points to his own 'word' or his 'teaching' or 'commandment'. The prologue of the Gospel (1:1–14) indicates that this is God's eternal word. The content of this word is defined unequivocally by Jesus himself: it is *love*. John 15:17 underlines it in a rather quaint grammatical construction: '*These things* (*tauta*, in the plural) I command you: *to love* one another'; i.e. 'these are *all the things* that matter, and all of them are only one: to love one another!'. The central episode of the washing of the feet of the disciples is meant to convey the same 'word' (John 13:1–20). When the epistles insistently repeat that 'he who loves is born of God' and he who does not love 'does not know God', they are not adding anything new but simply stating the same message of the Gospel: to be in Christ and to love are not two things but one single thing, which can be described either by looking at the root and the possibility of such a new life—the fact that God has sent his own Son—or by looking at the operation and reality of this new life—that we love one another.

(3) What is love? The interpreters of John who were misled by a supposedly Hellenising tendency in the author have interpreted Johannine love in mystical terms: love would be the spirit's aspiration towards the divine. A reading of the actual texts soon dispels this interpretation. Love is for John clearly a historical course of action which has to do with our relationship with actual human beings. Following the prophetic tradition, John does not hesitate in equating 'love' and 'justice' (1 John 2:29 and 4:7, 1 John 3:10). Moreover, Jesus points to his own actions as the paradigm of love, and uses the technical rabbinical expression 'good works' (for instance, 10:32–34). In fact, the controversy about 'the works' of Jesus is a central element in John's gospel. Love, the commandment of Christ, the works which he performed, are one and the same thing. And they refer concretely to the kinds of actions in the list reproduced in Matthew 25 (feeding the hungry, giving water to the thirsty, clothing the naked,

visiting the sick and imprisoned, etc.).[7] 1 John 3:17-18 makes the point in a terse and pointed way: 'But if anyone has this world's goods and sees his brother in need, yet closes his heart against him, *how does God's love abide in him?* Little children, let us not love in word or speech but in deed and in truth.'

The message of John is no different from that of the prophets. Neither of them contemplates the possibility of a theoretical, abstract, contemplative 'knowledge of God'. To know God is equivalent to coming actively to grips with God's concrete demands and actions. Knowing God is being involved in his invitations, commands, judgments. In theological terms—as we shall see later on—we can say that there is no relation to God outside a covenant, an active engagement, the specific content of which is defined by God himself in his own action which seals and ratifies the covenant. John—and the rest of the New Testament—tells us that the eternal purpose and content of this covenant has been once for all revealed and affirmed in Jesus Christ: the word of the covenant is the word of active love for one's neighbour (in the specific forms which respond to human needs and which can also be embraced by the term 'justice'). 'He who loves [his neighbour, as the context makes clear] knows God'. The reason is simple and definitive: 'because God is love'. The character of the knowledge is determined by the object: the God of the covenant, in whom 'the orphan finds refuge', 'who practises mercy and judgment', who is himself active love, cannot be known except by becoming totally committed to and involved in his own action.

The identity of the Lord and theology

The conclusions to which we have been driven by this brief Biblical study are of immense significance for theology. They require, in fact, a rethinking of the whole approach to theological thinking which is characteristic of our Western academic theology. Miranda is absolutely right when he says: 'the task of theology is not to enunciate truths but to proclaim the truth that is called "gospel".'[8] And he is also right in pointing out that the substitution of the former for the latter task has permitted the creation of an 'objective theology' which builds for itself a universe of abstractions and leaves the world untouched. We cannot now discuss the whole scope of the transformation that this needed reversal would mean, but a few systematic remarks may be in order.

(1) One may wonder why these seemingly obvious Biblical insights have so frequently eluded the exegetes and theologians (although, fortunately, they have always been clear to many a Christian). The answer seems to be that, in the process of its adaptation to the Graeco-Roman world, Christian theology (as part of a total movement through which the Church was co-opted into society) came to be more and more the prisoner of the idealistic Greek theology which had developed out of the work of the Greek philosophers. The criticism of the 'gods' of Greek mythology which these philosophers had undertaken, had issued in a 'purified' idea of 'the essence of the gods', a 'deity', prior and superior to the anthropomorphic gods of their pantheon. Such an essence could be known through philosophical speculation – basically through meditation on the higher forms of human speculative thought. Some of the early Greek Christian theologians subjected the God of the Bible to the same 'purifying' procedure. To be sure, Marcion's honest recognition that the Yahweh of the Old Testament would not lend himself to such a purification was rejected. This means that Yahweh was not accepted in his proper identity; through allegoric interpretation and philosophical distillation, his disturbing concreteness was concealed behind an eternal 'essence'. Liberal theology, whether idealistic, Kantian or existentialist, has carried this purification to its logical conclusion. The fundamental presupposition is always the same: there is an essence of God which we can know through philosophical speculation, moral conscience or mystical contemplation, before meeting the specific manifestations and concrete demands in which God comes – and has come – to us.[9] It is only natural that, when these philosophies prove untenable, and the 'essence' of God vanishes, we shall have a theology 'of the death of God', the Christian faith will be reduced to some form of philanthropic activity and Jesus left hanging in the air as an example.

(2) This perversion of the Biblical doctrine of God has, at least, two momentous consequences. The first is that God (should we not say 'the Lord' or even 'Yahweh' to avoid all confusion) is robbed of his particular identity. He is no longer the 'I am' who himself defines his own identity, he who is what he wants to be for us and for the world. He becomes objectified in our thought, apart from his own action. We make an image apart from his *debarim* (the 'words' and commandments in which he has defined the conditions of his covenant) and this is precisely what is forbidden in the second commandment! This introduces immediately a second consequence: it is precisely the characteristic of the Lord that he manifests his identity by announcing an action which involves man in an active relationship with his neighbour and with the world. There is no manifestation of God in Scripture in which a specific form of action is not included. God does not speak merely to inform or to notify: he speaks in order to invite, to command, to forbid a certain course of action. And this action is always related to a particular historical content—to men, nations, things, events.

(3) We shall have to ask ourselves later on how this call and invitation operate in relation to ourselves, who listen to God's call to the covenant through a historical mediation (the testimony of the prophets and the apostles). I do not claim that this is an easy question. But it would be totally wrong to approach it from the idealistic point of view which has dominated so much Christian theology and ethics. Obedience is not a *consequence* of our knowledge of God, just as it is not a pre-condition for it: obedience is included in our knowledge of God. Or, to put it more bluntly: obedience *is* our knowledge of God. There is not a separate *noetic* moment in our relationship to God. There is an imperfect faith, a faltering faith, but there cannot be, in the nature of the case, a *believing* disobedience—unless it is the 'dead faith' of which James speaks, and which 'profits nothing'. This is what is meant by emphasising the intrinsic demand for Christian truth to become historical, to be 'truth in the facts'. We do not know God in the abstract and then deduce from his essence some consequences. We know God in the synthetic act of responding to his demands.

(4) His demand is a particular course of action involving our neighbours and the world. How do we arrive at the definition of this course of action? How do we hear God's invitation today? We have already seen that the Bible does not leave us in darkness in this respect. The God of the covenant has himself designed a pattern of action which such words as justice, righteousness, the protection of the poor, active love, help us to discern. How is such discernment related to such forms of analysis, ideology and philosophy as Marxism or others which intend to indicate the texture and dynamics of historical life? We shall have to return to this question in several contexts. It may be that we shall have to criticise, correct or reject the way in which some Christians in Latin America are responding to these questions. What on Biblical grounds we cannot do is to refuse their challenge to concrete, historical obedience.

Historical verification! When the Baptist asks from jail whether Jesus is or is not the Messiah, he is not offered a theoretical answer or an iron-clad argument. He is only confronted with facts: 'the blind receive sight and the lame walk, lepers are cleansed, the dead are raised up and the poor have good news preached to them' (Matthew 11:4–5). Historical verification! We may conclude with two quotations. One is the well known last thesis of Marx on Feuerbach: 'Until now the philosophers have only interpreted the world in various ways; the point is to change it.' The second is perhaps less known, but no less disturbing. It comes from Paul's First Letter to the Corinthians (4:19–20): 'I will come to you soon . . . and I will find out not the talk of these arrogant people but their power. For the Kingdom of God does not consist in talk but in power.'

CHAPTER III

THE OPIATE OF
THE PEOPLE

SOMEBODY HAS QUOTED a bit of Russian humour: 'Thank God that God does not exist! But what if, may God forbid, God does exist?' The contradictions which make the point of this saying bear a certain resemblance to the ambiguities that we find today within the Marxist camp concerning religion in general and Christianity in particular. This is the subject that we want to explore in this chapter. Our purpose in doing so is not merely academic. From the point of view of a Christian concerned with active obedience in a historical situation—and, as I understand it, obedience here means participation in an effort to change the structures which create oppression and misery—the main question is whether and to what extent the Marxist criticism of religion can help us to expose the shortcomings or betrayals in our obedience and to correct our attitudes. At the same time, Christians who have embarked together with Marxists in a common struggle are entitled to know the attitude that their partners take and the evaluation they make concerning what for Christians is essential and non-negotiable, namely their faith in Jesus Christ. We must, therefore, ask two questions: one, concerning the nature and significance of the Marxist critique of religion; the other, about the present stance of Marxists in relation to the Christian faith.

Marx: religion as economics and economics as religion

In order to elucidate the original Marxist critique of religion

I will briefly focus on Marx himself (with only brief mention of other thinkers). This for two reasons. On the one hand, we find in Marx more clearly than in any Marxist, both the depth and the ambiguity of the Marxist criticism. On the other hand, more than anybody else, he articulates this criticism within the political and economic discussions, and in doing so, brings up precisely those aspects which prove more significant in our search for an authentic and efficacious Christian obedience. It is also for this reason that I shall discuss Marx's political and economic criticism of Christianity before dealing—much more briefly—with his better known philosophical writings on this question.

Two famous quotations from 1843—the year which marks Marx's shift from a liberal to a socialist perspective, from the censorship of expression in Prussia to a freer press in France—places us in the centre of his criticism of religion. One is the opening sentence of his 'Contribution to the Critique of Hegel's Philosophy of Right': 'For Germany, the *criticism of religion* is essentially complete, and the criticism of religion is the premise (*Voraussetzung*) of all criticism'.[1] The second quotation is from a letter to his friend Ruge explaining his reason for leaving the *Rheinische Zeitung*, the liberal journal which he had edited in Cologne: 'I asked ... that religion be criticised through a criticism of the political situation, rather than that the political situation be criticised through religion.'[2] Prior to these writings, we have the articles concerning freedom of the press, the feudal laws against the stealing of wood, and other matters directed against the Prussian confessional state. Following the writings quoted, we come to 'On the Jewish Question' and the Paris Manuscripts, where we move towards the articulation of historical materialism. Running the risk of oversimplification, I shall try to summarise Marx's argument at this decisive point.

1. The aristocratic Prussian state presents itself as a Christian state, as a bulwark against moral and religious dissolution. Marx immediately sees through this use of religion as a screen and justification for the feudal order:

> ... in their hands religion acquires a polemical bitterness impregnated with political tendencies and becomes, in a more

or less conscious manner, simply a sacred cloak to hide desires which are both very secular and at the same time very imaginary.[3]

Several points deserve observation: (a) Marx denounces the appeal to religion as ideological—it is only 'a cloak' which, perhaps unconsciously, hides the real purpose of the policy, namely the preservation of aristocratic feudal power. It is also contradictory, because the true essence of the Christian religion, to which they appeal, is universal and therefore cannot be realised on the basis of the exclusive claims of a confessional state: it could only be realised in a state based on something which is universal, i.e. on reason itself. Finally, it is hypocritical, because it pretends to impregnate all of life with the demands of the Christian religion ('if somebody, out of pure religiosity, becomes allied with religion, he is compelled to hand over to it the decision on all matters'[4]), while clearly the Prussian state does not intend to comply with the Biblical teaching about renouncing property, turning the other cheek or refusing to be drawn into public litigation, to cite only a few examples.[5]

(b) There is a deeper question. The religious justification of the state is illusory because mankind has already overcome the religious view of itself in which such a justification might have been significant: the objective conditions for such a use of religion are no longer present. We can leave aside for the time being the accuracy of such a claim. What Marx is here alluding to is the philosophical criticism of religion, particularly as formulated by men like Feuerbach, which had exposed religion as man's own creation,[6] the expression of man's search for himself. Any meaning which Christianity may have, as the highest form or religion,[7] is to be found therefore in its universality, its understanding of universal humanity, which is achieved by projecting generic humanity on to the divine in the myth of Jesus Christ as the God-man. However it is not in a confessional state, but in the rational, atheist, state where this idea of universal humanity finds its best expression. We must, therefore, find in such a state the true fulfilment of 'the human basis of the Christian religion.'[8] We have here the view which Feuerbach

44

had expressed in a classical form: God is the projection of man's unrealised humanity, of his creativity and perfection. Atheism, by removing this false screen, returns man to his humanity — it is the fulfilment in reality of what was realised in religion in an illusory form. Marx sees the liberal state as the concrete embodiment of this realisation. Religion is fulfilled in humanism, and humanism in the secular state.

(c) It is, nevertheless, important to point out that, even in this highly philosophical formulation, Marx was aware of waging a concrete political battle. The struggle for a free press, for liberal legislation, the criticism of the state, were the ways through which men could achieve this rational existence which corresponds to their true essence.

2. In the discussion with his erstwhile collaborator B. Bauer in 'The Jewish Question', Marx pushes his argument one step further: to the criticism of politics and the liberal state — this very state in which Christianity was both taken up and overcome. The fact is that the liberal state functions exactly like religion: it dichotomises man into an ideal projection, 'the citizen', in which rationality, justice, equality are (idealistically) realised, but the real man continues to live in the world of inequality, injustice and egoism, 'so that people, equals in the heavenly sphere of their political world, were unequal in the earthly existence of society: just as Christians are equal in Heaven but unequal on earth'.[9]

(a) The ideological function of this 'theology' of the state is unmercifully unmasked in the criticism of the North American and French 'democratic' constitutions: the vaunted freedom is only a cover for the unrestricted expansion of individualistic egoism — the freedom to practise one's religion, to acquire and accumulate property, to trade and profit free from interferences, not in solidarity but in self-seeking. Whatever limitations there may be, they will result only from the mutual checks of individual egoisms conflicting with each other. 'The real man is recognised only under the form of the egoistic *individual*; true man, only under the form of the *abstract citizen*'.[10]

(b) Marx understands the criticism of the state as the extension of the criticism of religion, 'the unmasking of the non-sacred forms of human alienation':[11]

> The members of the political state are religious because of the dualism between the life of the individual and the life of humanity [generic] ... in the sense that man considers this political life which is beyond his own individuality to be his real life.[12] ... This is a figment of the imagination, a dream, the postulate of Christianity, the sovereignty of man, but of man as a being absolutely different from the real man.[13]

The atheist state does not emancipate man; it merely transfers his alienation. There is liberation only in the dissolution of such a state, in the elimination of this new religion in a communist society.

3. But there is still more, a more fundamental alienation within bourgeois society. In the work we are quoting, Marx contrasts the 'religious' Jew with the 'real Jew' — the man who has been engendered by his particular history in Europe. His characterisation represents a gross historical misconstruction. But this error — which in other respects has had negative consequences — is not very important concerning our subject because what Marx is describing as 'the spirit of the practical Jew' is really bourgeois Christianity. What is the essence of this spirit?

> Money is the jealous God of Israel, before which no other God can legitimately stand ... Money is the general *value* of all things, constituted in itself ... It has deprived everything else of all value, both in the world of nature and in the world of man. Money is the essence of work and of the existence of man alienated from himself and this estranged essence dominates him and is worshipped by him. The God of the Jews has been secularised, he has become a universal God. The bill of exchange [*Wechsel*] is the real god of the Jew. His god is only an imaginary bill of exchange.[14]

Only twenty years later, in the first book of *Das Kapital*, will

46

Marx be able to analyse in detail, in his discussion of 'The fetishism of commodities', the mechanism of this 'theological transaction' which he identifies metaphorically in the earlier work. There is no possibility of discussing here in detail this notion that, far from being accidental, is the very heart of Marx's most mature and elaborated work. In a simplified way, we can state it as follows: (a) as soon as any commodity is not used immediately to fulfil a human need, but as trade—for instance, a pound of rice is exchanged for a piece of wood—it takes on a new quality: the apparent ability to 'measure' or to 'represent' another commodity: we say that a pound of rice is equivalent to such and such amount of wood; (b) this idea is, in fact, a distortion, because what this commodity really represents is the work (the amount of human effort and time—the investment of human life and energy) required for its production; (c) this masking becomes even more disguised when a particular kind of commodity, namely money, is invested with the capacity to measure value as something inherent in itself—actually the only meaning of money is this acquired, conventional, humanly created capacity to represent human work *as if it belonged to it*: in fact, the value does not reside in the thing itself but in the valuation ascribed to it; man invests it with value (the value of his work) and thus this work which confers value is objectified as if it were a quality of the thing; (d) the culmination of this process is ascribing to this fictional representation a creative ability, the capacity to grow and to reproduce itself, 'thus projecting before men the social character of their own work as if it were a material character of the products of their work';[15] (e) the best way to understand the process is to see it in the light of fetishism, the act through which man invests the qualities of life and power in an image which he has made himself.[16] Capitalism, therefore, which is precisely the cult of this hypostatisation, the cult of money, is the perfect form of religion: it robs man of this relation to himself, to his neighbour, to the world by mediating it through this fetishistic creation, money.

4. We will have to ask the question about the status of these analogies to religion—the state, money—in Marx's thought. But I want first to call attention to still another side of his struggle

against religion: his rejection of 'religious communism'. The attempt to base a communist programme on Biblical or Christian sources was by no means absent in Marx's and Engels's time. In fact, one could say that, particularly in France but also in Germany, it had preceded Marxism in a strict sense. One would expect the leaders of the proletarian revolution to welcome the co-operation of these Christians who wholeheartedly supported their programme and offered to bring to it the enthusiasm and fervour that a religious commitment can create. Marx's and Engels's position is, nevertheless, adamant; there is no possible co-operation. The 'Letter against Kriege' is the most elaborate statement of this opposition.[17] (a) A moral transposition of communism by an appeal to Christian love is doubly deceptive: on the one hand, Christian love is not a real human relationship but an imaginary relationship of non-existent 'religious selves' — in fact, Christian love has been able to express itself in the existing situation of alienation and misery without changing it. Christian love does not change the real situation; it only sublimates it. On the other hand, it makes communism appear as the generous work of those who, from within their already achieved humanity, condescend to help the poor and needy. (b) Everything becomes mystified in this religious communism. The class-enemy is made into a heretic, the struggle takes on the religious intolerance of a crusade and the enemy the hazy character of a sinner. The domination of money is made into a religious question, 'the cult of Mammon'. Once the concrete character of the problem has been thus confused, the revolution becomes a voluntaristic, moralistic, utopian or anarchic upheaval, a mere revolt. The proletariat is assimilated to 'the lamb of God', a mythological image which can hardly preside over a realistic historical struggle. (c) What Kriege is really espousing is communion, an old German and philosophical dream 'which is in direct opposition to communism'.

It would not be difficult to point out several contradictions in these arguments. In fact, Marx himself has more than once used the religious and enthusiastic language which he rejects here. But it is not my purpose now to argue this point. Rather, I would like to receive the criticism as a valid warning against the self-deception and confusion which so easily creep into a political programme of any sort when it is clothed in religious language. To this we shall return later on. On the other hand, I want to point out the strength of the anti-religious ethos in the whole Marxist tradition, beginning with its founder. Sixty odd years later, Lenin will be just as relentless in the rejection of 'religious communists' in the Russian revolution.

5. We are left with the hard task of asking whether there is unity in this complex of criticisms. It is, in one sense, part of the vaster problem now raging among Marxists and marxologists of different persuasions: how are we to understand the relation between the different stages in the development of Marx's thought? Without attempting to argue the point, I am taking the common-sense view that a sound interpretation will try to take into account both continuity and discontinuity in this development. More particularly, I think that one must follow a two-way street: from the early to the more mature form of his thought in order to discover progress and continuity, and from the latter to the former in order to spot change and discontinuity. When we follow this method, it seems to me that two conclusions become clear concerning our subject:

(a) The religious element is seen always as an ideological screen, as a false consciousness of a real human need. As an ideology, it hides from man the real nature of his alienation. On the one hand, it offers a false remedy to man's sickness—a future or transcendent heaven of peace and unity in which man alienates his human force and thus is lulled into accepting his present real hell. Marx is caustic in the denunciation of this deleterious function of religion. One need only quote one among many of his penetrating comments: 'The mortgage that the peasant holds on heavenly goods is his guaranty for the mortgage that the bourgeoisie has on the earthly goods of the peasant.'[18] On the other hand, religion invests the present misery with a sacred character: it is the 'opiate of the people' in the negative sense of putting them to sleep.[19] This is the understanding on which a more militant attitude against religion has found its basis in communist anti-religious propaganda. Lenin leans to this interpretation, as is evident from his adaptation of Marx's

49

famous dictum: Lenin speaks of religion as an 'opiate *for* the people'.[20] It is, as we shall see, the point of view predominant in the communist parties belonging to the Third International.

(b) It is nevertheless clear that this interpretation, which projects on the later Marx the philosophical anti-religious mood of some of his earlier writings, cannot be the controlling perspective. This, for several reasons: (i) It is not his original contribution: it can be found both in the French and in the German atheistic movements; (ii) Marx himself took exception to these movements, not because he conceded any value to religion but because this atheism was still 'too religious': it tried to combat religion as if it were something in itself, while it is only the reflected image of man's real alienation rooted in the material conditions of production; (iii) consequently, the real criticism must be carried to the political and even more to the economic realm: a reflected consciousness will change when the material conditions which originated it are changed; (iv) this corresponds to Marx's understanding of the function of criticism: it is the theoretical effort to lay bare the conditions under which certain situations obtain in order that men can undertake effective action. The criticism of religion is valuable in so far as it is a criticism of bourgeois society which unveils its dynamics and provides the revolutionary proletariat with adequate theoretical instruments for carrying out its historical mission of destroying and overcoming this society.

In this sense Althusser is right in pointing out the movement from ideological to scientific thought as the driving force in Marx's development. In a very simple sense—following previous thinking—Marx sees religion as emerging (in primitive societies where economic fetishism is not yet at work) as a response to the mystery of forces which man has not yet been able to understand or dominate. In this sense, the progress of science naturally displaces religion. When social conditions become more complex and economic alienation emerges, separating man from his work —and therefore from his relation to himself, other men and nature—religion becomes the projection of a unity which has been lost. This process reaches its perfect manifestation (which is the complete perversion of reality) in the fetishism of money (the total alienation of work) and in Christianity, particularly in Protestantism (the wholly individualistic projection of man's life into a transcending realm). It is therefore only through a scientific disclosure of the real mechanism of this alienation — the process of production, surplus value, capitalistic accumulation — that man can be given back the possibility of controlling his relation to work (and therefore to himself, his neighbour and his world) and thus to make religion unnecessary. This is the reason why scientific political action is the real criticism of religion. The proletariat must not waste its forces in a useless and diversionary battle against religion. But it is also for this reason that all attempts to 'mystify' the struggle by appealing to a religious communism must be strenuously resisted: it would short-circuit precisely that element which alone can resolve the contradiction, namely a scientific understanding of the dynamics of historical change. It would introduce at the heart of the communist movement a powerful element of occultation and confusion: the imaginary religious solution to the contradiction in which man is involved.

If this interpretation is correct, we are still faced with several problems. One is posed by the way in which Marx's criticism of religion has been reinterpreted in diverging ways within Marxism itself. A second one concerns the status of the analogies to religion which Marx keeps using at decisive points in his later, more scientific work. Finally, there is the question concerning the extent to which his criticism is valid and justified from a historical point of view and how we are to evaluate it from a theological and Biblical perspective. The first question we shall briefly address in this chapter; the last two we shall leave for the next.

Between rejection and openness

Traditional communist attitudes towards religion are well known. A recent French Marxist handbook — quite up-to-date and discerning in other areas — serves this anti-religious menu in almost grotesque expressions: 'Marxism is against all religion . . .'; 'Marxist philosophy . . . explains religion totally in terms of the economic and social infrastructure . . .'; 'religion, openly combated under the dictatorship of the proletariat, will vanish of itself during the communist phase and will disintegrate as a false idol' with the progress of science. Even more ridiculous, the author enumerates 'Marxist teachings concerning the origins of Christianity' in a strange concoction of the theses of the Tübingen School and the amateurish works of Engels and Kautsky—as if there had been no historical and Biblical scholarship during the last hundred years.[21] A visit to any communist library would yield scores of quotations in the same vein.

Such rejection reflects the attitude of the traditional Communist parties of the Third International, subject to the orientation of the USSR. It corresponds also to the practice of the two major socialist countries: the Soviet Union and the People's Republic of China. While both have in theory proclaimed religious freedom and defined religion as a private question in which the state does not interfere, in practice, organised religion has suffered severe limitations amounting in some cases to open persecution. In China, the churches have been virtually eliminated from public life. In the Soviet Union and some of the Eastern European countries, several forms of discrimination in social, educational and political life have been enforced against clergy and people manifesting religious allegiance. There is scarcely any need to document these facts which have been amply reported—not without exaggeration and bias—in the Western press. The ambiguity of a proclamation of religious freedom and the practice of anti-religious discrimination can be traced back to Lenin himself when he discusses the status of religion in the socialist state. While he considers religion a private matter from the point of view of the state, he insists that 'the party of the proletariat *demands* from the state that it declare religion a private thing, but it does not for a moment consider the struggle against the opiate of the people to be "a private thing" . . .'[22] Yet it is clear that such a neat distinction between the state and the party does not obtain in reality and therefore the 'ideological battle' of the party becomes in fact anti-religious discrimination and even persecution in the totality of public life.

In this respect it is significant to note that as late as 1963, when de-Stalinisation was already in full swing, the Central Committee of the Communist Party in the USSR received the famous 'Illitchev Report' calling for a renewal and intensification of anti-religious propaganda and repeating all the traditional arguments against religion as anti-scientific and reactionary.[23] Discounting as merely tactical or opportunistic all changes in the churches, he rejects all compromises with religion and concludes: 'By its very spirit, its nature, the objective meaning of its dogmas, religion remains, under all conditions, an anti-scientific ideology, foreign to communism.'

He then invites a wholesale attack on religion, using all means available short of violence, abuse or brutality. The primary aim is the education of children and young people. For this purpose, it is necessary to co-ordinate all efforts:

> Only by co-ordinating all the means and all the forms of our ideological work shall we obtain success. We must remember that the best decisions concerning atheist education will remain a dead letter if we lack persevering work or organisation.

> We must be alert against the mistake of considering atheist propaganda as just one more campaign. It is one of the strategic points in the ideological front. Success on the total front in the formation of a scientific concept of the world and of a communist morality among the Soviet people, the formation of a new man, will depend on our activity.

Not only was this report favourably received, but from the highest Soviet authority, Nikita Kruschev, we hear the insistence on the need to emphasise the education of youth in order to prevent it from falling prey to 'moral deformations', among which those deriving from religion occupy an important place.[24] The official Programme of the Party states:

> ... the Party employs the means of ideological influence in order to educate men according to the spirit of a scientific and materialistic view of the world, in order to overcome religious prejudices, although without hurting the feelings of the believers. It is necessary patiently to explain the inconsistencies of religious beliefs, which originated in earlier times

when man was subject to the blind forces of nature and to the yoke of society, due to the ignorance of the true causes of the natural and social phenomena.[25]

The Italian Communist Party has been the first to challenge this monolithic intransigence. The peculiar conditions of the Italian situation, where many Christians were active in the resistance against Fascism, as partisans during the World War II and in the effort to build a democratic society afterwards, provided the occasion for close co-operation with Marxists, leading to a revision of some of the traditional anti-religious tenets. Already Gramsci, the brilliant founder of the party, had seen that a revolution was impossible in Italy without taking into account both the political strength and the popular influence of the Catholic Church. While most communist parties still today refuse membership to Christians, the Italian Communist Party wrote already in 1945 in its Constitution that any citizen may join the party 'regardless of race, *religious faith or philosophical convictions*' as long as he accepts the political programme of the party. The communist leader Palmiro Togliatti, in a speech in 1954, underlines that mankind is faced today with the problem of war, in which all the values of civilisation are threatened, and invites Christians and Marxists to work together for the survival of those humanist values which both traditions cherish. But only at the X Congress of the Italian Communist Party will the necessary theoretical presupposition of this appeal and co-operation be fully developed:

Today our concern is not limited to eliminate the obstacles and sectarianism that prevent co-operation between socialist and Catholic forces for the achievement of the most immediate economic and political results. We have to understand that the aspiration for a socialist society can not only find a place among men who have a religious faith but that *it can also find a stimulus in the religious conscience itself* confronted with the dramatic problems of the contemporary world.[26]

In a speech in Bergamo shortly after, Togliatti went even further, affirming that even in a future classless society there would be place for a religious consciousness, not only as a remnant of the past, but also as contributing to the development of a new future.[27]

The positions officially defined by the Italian party correspond to the same historical, pragmatic approach that we find in Fidel Castro and Ernesto (Ché) Guevara. They discover many common humanistic concerns among Marxists and Christians. They further encounter a number of Christians joining in the struggle for a new, socialist society: they simply draw the conclusion that the Christian faith does not *necessarily* generate a reactionary or anti-revolutionary position and that, in fact, it may and at times does stimulate a revolutionary attitude. The Italian Marxist thinker Lucio Lombardo Radice claims that such a revision of the traditional positions in view of the new facts belongs to the most authentic Marxist conception. He rejects the view of Illitchev, for whom all changes among Christians are only tactical manoeuvres in order to survive in a time of social revolution and concludes that—whatever explanation the Marxist may give to it—'there is also an authentic revolutionary impulse in religious faith'.[28]

Neither Radice nor Togliatti was led by the revision of the classical Marxist view of the role of religion to reinterpret the basic philosophical premises of dialectical and historical materialism. Several Marxist philosophers have, in fact, offered a positive view of Christianity by reinterpreting it in radical immanent terms as mythical or symbolic expression of a humanist ethos.[29] But the problem lies elsewhere: if Christians, who hold fast to their faith in a personal, transcendent God, are admitted to a political party which rests on the acceptance of Marxism-Leninism, should 'atheism', traditionally considered a constitutive element in the ideology, be seen as a dispensable part of it, so to say an optional article of the creed? This is what several Christian interpreters of Marxism have suggested. The Italian Catholic Giulio Girardi, for instance, has argued that atheism is not for Marxism a 'fundamental thesis', i.e. one on which the rest is built, but only a negative statement of the absolute value of man over against a diminution of man which would be implicit in the acceptance of God. If the disjunctive God/man should prove false, atheism would cease to be necessary for Marxism.[30]

Is this interpretation possible? The French Marxist Roger Garaudy, in his postscript to Girardi's work has accepted this interpretation and, in later works, has developed it positively.[31] He even welcomes the correction to what he calls 'Marxist distortions' which comes from Christian faith. Building on a criticism of the deformations which socialism has suffered, Garaudy believes that the radical prophetic questioning of all human achievement, while it can be a deterrent to action—an opiate—can also keep open, when it is coupled with an historical engagement, the growing edge of deeper transformations and further progress in the struggle against man's alienation. In this sense, what Péguy has called 'a crack for grace' may be necessary in order to prevent further hardening within the Marxist revolutionary movements. Marxists would be wrong in transforming Marx's criticism of religion into a philosophical dogma: 'it is a historical analysis of social contradictions and their ideological projections'. Atheism cannot be demanded as a confession: at most it can be justified as a methodological principle excluding supernatural explanations for natural phenomena. But there is in human life and in historical movements a wide field which cannot be reduced to scientific explanation: artistic creation, love, faith. A true revolution cannot be realised unless such depths in human life are taken into account. The co-operation of Christians who hold to their faith with Marxists is indispensable for such a task. 'There is a Christian Stalinism just as there is a Marxist clericalism' which must be rejected: we can only overcome our perversions 'through this constant mutual questioning on the basis of all that each one of our communities has at its best'.

What are we to do with these radically different interpretations? Should we understand them as accommodation, opportunism, a change of attitude, real discrepancies of interpretations, a tactical game? It seems to me that we must take three facts into account. Firstly, the original sources of Marxism are not unambiguous. Though none of the classics of Marxism was favourable to religion, the nature, emphasis and weight of their criticism is by no means univocal. We have already seen some oscillations in Marx's own thought; but the situation is much more complex when we introduce other early Marxists. Henry Desroches very soberly summarises the problem:

> We have observed that Engels' atheism functions very differently from that of Marx and we could observe that what they have in common cannot be identified either with the *atheisms* observable in the socialist descendants which bear their name or with the socialisms or socialists who sometimes accept their analyses or their economic-political programmes but which have nevertheless rejected either their theory or their strategy concerning the recession of religion.[32]

Secondly, these variations should not be isolated as theoretical positions, but should be seen in the perspective of the historical situations in which they arose: to this we shall return in the next chapter. And thirdly, these differences must also be placed in the context of the different trends and the theoretical and practical discussions to be found today within Marxism. When all this is done, we emerge, I think, with a clearer understanding both of the significance, the limitations and the possible value of the Marxist criticism of religion for a Christian who wants to take seriously his place and responsibility as such in the world of today.

CHAPTER IV

THE BIBLICAL CRITICISM
OF RELIGION

THE RATHER COMPLEX and theoretical nature of the questions
we have been discussing should not hide from us their immediate
bearing on our main concern: the historical obedience of
Christians in today's world. To put it very simply, Marx has been
telling us that Christian religion has been, is and will be a sign
of man's sickness, a diversion from his true human vocation and
an instrument of his oppression. When man comes of age, when
he develops his productive forces and his awareness, he takes
control of history and discards this, now unnecessary, illusion.
It is my contention that a Christian, when confronted with this
challenge, should not hasten to refute it, but should rather ask
himself how can he understand it, what it is that he is being told
about himself and his community. As Christians we are not
judged by Marx or Marxism; one alone is our judge: the Lord.
But Marx is a witness. And he witnesses against us precisely at
those points where we have received a very definite responsibility:
love, justice, abundant life for all men, the responsibility for
creation and the world, the care of the poor. We must try to
understand his accusation.

Where are the Christians?

Orthodox Marxism has done much to obscure the discussion by
presenting Marx's view as a sort of new—atheistic—metaphysics,

a series of doctrinal statements about the nature of religion (and many other subjects). As a matter of fact, Marx's writings should be understood, in the first place, as an attempt to analyse the specific conditions and relations obtaining in a particular society and to abstract from this analysis a 'theory' which can and should be tested against other societies and epochs and, to the extent that it proves true, be used to guide and illuminate a course of action which corresponds to the dynamics of historical change. In fact, it has sometimes been noted that his analyses prove all the more accurate when they refer to this more immediate situation: the rising of the bourgeoisie and the Industrial Revolution, and become more and more questionable the further he goes back into history—as for instance when he talks of the 'Asiatic mode of production' or of 'primitive communism'. This general observation is important when we deal with his criticism of religion. We should not see it *primarily* as a general denunciation of religion as such—this is indeed a secondary, unoriginal and quite questionable generalisation—but as a very specific exposure of the ideological function of the Christian religion, and particularly of Protestantism, in relation to the individualistic, egoistic and profit-crazy bourgeois world. It seems further that the criticism of bourgeois Christianity is for us a fundamental task, not as a masochistic exercise or a new pharisaical beating of the breast, but as a necessary effort at self-understanding in order to purify our obedience. It is necessary, moreover, because further psycho-social insight, not available to Marx, has even strengthened and sharpened this criticism.

There is the basic fact of the active opposition which the workers who began to claim their rights at the beginnings of the industrial era found in the organised churches. If we wish to know what kind of Christian preaching Marx could find in his own country, we need only to listen to the instructions given by the preacher at the court of Potsdam:

> ... what matters is to stimulate the attachment to the old constitution, to alert the people against a freedom and an equality applied to themselves, to show the need for differences between social conditions and to lend influence and authority

to our words by means of intelligent allusions to the consequences of the furious passion for freedom of the French Revolution.[1]

Was Marx so far off the mark when he scornfully pointed out that the 'Christian principles' defended by the Prussian councillors 'preach the necessity of a ruling and an oppressed class'?[2] 'Where was the pulpit' pointedly asks Gollwitzer, where worker leaders like the tailor Weitling or the mechanic Bebel 'would not be told that the attitude desired by God was submission to their lot as a humble recognition of God's order?'[3] At most, they would have heard the echoes of feeble exhortations to the rich and powerful to be lenient and benevolent in their dealings . . . lest they create the dreaded conditions of disorder. Girardi's conclusion is by no means exaggerated: 'Whenever the working class expressed its aspirations and demands, the Church stood with the opposition, against the workers. The workers grew up, therefore, considering the Church as their class enemy.'[4] No doubt there are exceptions to this judgment: there are also exceptions in the attitude of the socialist movement towards Christianity. But in so far as the organised churches as a whole are concerned, and as a global impact of the official Christian attitude, the verdict is unquestionable.

The break of the working classes with Christianity was not always so dramatic. In most cases, the emerging proletariat found that the Church had simply nothing to say to them, no meaningful message that spoke to their conditions. They silently left the churches. As Dirks says, Christ 'had become invisible, and his word was not heard any more'.[5] In order to change that situation it would have been necessary that 'Christians would have entered their sphere of existence through the strength of Christian self-denying service'.[6] But this did not happen, and so a whole class, the *avant-garde* of the new world in Marx's analysis, became totally estranged from the churches. Perhaps they did not so much become militantly anti-Christian (after all, militant atheism is a phenomenon of the intellectuals in the liberal bourgeoisie) as impervious to the voice of Christianity. Marx simply registered and articulated this reality: religion is an instrument of the oppressing classes; the workers have no more use for it. This may not be true as a final diagnosis; it was true enough, unfortunately, in relation to what the churches represented in his time.

Marx had once paid Luther and the Reformation a sort of left-handed compliment. He credited them with having liberated man's conscience from external (religious) authority. But he added that in so doing, they bound man to his chains precisely through this same conscience. Luther, he says, 'overcame bondage out of *devotion* by replacing it with bondage out of *conviction*'.[7] In so doing, he simply gave expression to the sort of human consciousness that corresponds to the needs of rising capitalism and the bourgeoisie: they do not any longer need men who are kept in physical slavery through external compulsion, rather they require an individual kept subject internally and by conviction to the conditions of the modern industrial chain of production. Since those early observations of Marx and Engels, much has been written about the relationship between Protestantism and the rise of capitalism. Max Weber's classical thesis in this respect has been corrected and refined, but the basic fact of the existence of a mutual reinforcement and stimulation between them seems established beyond any doubt.

The fact of this relationship is not only confirmed but strengthened by the quite evident relation between the capitalist colonial and neo-colonial expansion into what is now called the 'Third World' and the missionary enterprise. The expansionist ideology is everywhere present in the early documents of the missionary societies and leaders: they understood themselves, not certainly as traders (and sometimes they were quite critical of their business compatriots), but truly as the spearhead of the modern, free, civilised (and Christian) world, dispelling the intellectual and spiritual darkness of the 'far off lands'. The churches that emerged from their work are frequently permeated with the values, spirit and goals of bourgeois capitalist culture. The result is quite often middle-class churches formed by people concerned with their individualistic (spiritual and social) promotion, having lost their solidarity with their nation and the class from which they arose, uncritically supporting the reactionary ideology of their (real or desired) social class. There is here an interplay of very different forces, and we must avoid the mistake of making the missionary enterprise responsible for imperialist expansion or for the emergence of bourgeois Christian groups. But at the same time we must be quite honest about the role that it has played and still plays in giving religious sanction, and integrating in a religious/ideological outlook the aspirations and needs of a reactionary social class.

Social psychology helps us to overcome one-sided schematisations by showing that the ideological function of religion is much more subtle and complex than we usually think. Engels had already noted that the error of ideology was its failure to discover the real motivation of man's behaviour by attributing it to certain ideas. He even says that this happens 'unconsciously', or 'with a false conscience'.[8] But it was Freud who has—more or less contemporaneously with Engels—shown how repressed drives or desires become an unconscious motivation, something that we do not recognise and therefore attribute to other factors. This happens (although Freud himself did not explore this area) not only individually but also socially. As Silva says, 'the social repression represented by ideology consists therefore in confusing real motivations . . . with apparent ones'.[9] On the other hand, Erich Fromm has shown how the objective conditions and subjective responses of the sixteenth and seventeenth centuries helped to create in Europe a 'social personality' that we can call bourgeois. The Protestant understanding of religious dependence and obedience, of discipline and perfection, its individualistic conception of man's relation to God and neighbour, corresponded to the needs and reflected the conditions of the newly emerging, competitive, impersonal society—itself in turn conditioned by the new organisation of production. Finally, in the Latin American continent, or among the black population in the USA, sociologists have exposed the different processes through which the oppressed were led to accept oppression by adopting the point of view of the dominant class, to internalise the oppressor's imposition of inferiority, to develop a slave-consciousness. When this happens, every religious performance and observance (however profound and liberating may have been its original intention) becomes in that context the carrier of oppression, an instrument of spiritual enslavement. Domination becomes a religiously founded fact; the bond of oppression is divinely sealed. Every religious act is a denial of one's own humanity. Only the severity of this judgment — however one might qualify it in detail — probes the depth of the problem.

Against this background we can easily see how religious faith can be used for reactionary purposes. It does not need to be a conscious use: it even functions better when it is practised unwittingly. Thus, Brazilian and Chilean generals are not aware of any internal contradiction in their attitude when they justify the torture and repression of their police state as the best, or the only way to safeguard 'Western Christian civilisation'. We cannot here take the space necessary to identify the different ways in which Christian doctrine is exploited in this respect: the ideas of peace and reconciliation, of God's order, the primacy of love, the Christian attitude of humility and dependence, the eschatological relativising of all human achievements, the symbol of the Crucified Saviour are only a few of the most obvious elements which are constantly manipulated in order to buttress the present oppressive system.

Christianity operates as a brake against revolution also by providing religious sanction to 'third alternatives' between capitalism and socialism. Christians are invited to take a position which is equidistant from both right and left, to reject both liberal individualism and totalitarian collectivism, to support both freedom and justice, personal development and social solidarity. Over against such an ideal, they display the record of suffering and injustice created by both capitalism and present forms of Marxist socialism. There is no doubt that one can make a good case for such a platform on Christian terms. But how can it become concrete? What are the forms of property, organisation of the people, process of development which are proposed? What is the strategy for overcoming economic and political dependence, or the oppression of the present power structures? Lacking an original understanding of the dynamics of the historical situation, these groups are usually led to adopt some mixture of socialist and capitalist measures. When these prove contradictory, the movement splinters: some move towards the socialist camp — and sometimes even become all the more fanatic and extreme, transferring to the ideology the religious fervour and the voluntaristic stubbornness of their Christian commitment. But the majority usually gravitates towards the traditional alliance with the right. Marx's rejection of 'religious socialism' seems to be partially justified by the history of 'Christian-progressive' parties.

God's demand and man's religion

For the reader of the Bible, the accusation that religion is used as a substitute for justice, as an attempt to make human oppression before man and God, does not come as a surprise. Such a denunciation is the constant theme of the prophetic witness. It hardly needs documentation, but a brief dossier may help to keep the fact before our eyes. There was a frequent misunderstanding in the religious life of Israel (by which usually the behaviour of the leaders is meant): the belief that real worship can coexist with injustice and oppression: 'Because my people approach me with their mouths and honour me with their lips, while their hearts are far from me'. (Isaiah 29:13). The contradiction lies, as the context makes clear, in injustice and oppression. The sentence is repeated in Ezekiel (33:31, 'their heart is set on selfish gain') contrasting their hypocritical praise with their real greed and egoism. A people who does not practise justice has forfeited the right to speak to Yahweh: '. . . yet they ask counsel of me day by day and say they delight in knowing my ways as if they were a nation that did righteousness'. (Isaiah 58:2).

In such a situation, religion has become a cloak to cover disobedience, and the religious leaders preside over this deception. Jeremiah (5:31; 7:9–10; 8:11), Micah (3:5), Ezekiel (13:10) repeat almost verbally the same accusation: false prophets keep talking about peace when there is no peace. How can there be peace when there is murder and extortion (Jeremiah), violence and fraud (Ezekiel), plunder of the poor (Micah)? Actually, there is a conspiracy of lies: 'Prophets prophesy lies and priests go hand in hand with them, and my people love to have it so'. (Jeremiah 5:31).

64

Such religion is only an excuse. Micah puts it in terms of a public hearing, taking the whole universe as witness. Israel plays the part of the pious worshipper. They ask, how much does God want? 'What shall I bring when I approach the Lord? Am I to approach him with whole-offerings or yearling calves? . . . Shall I offer my eldest son for my wrongdoings?' These are only excuses: 'You have already been told what is good . . . to act justly, to love loyally and to lead a humble life before your God' (Micah 6:6–8). Or in the words of Jesus: 'lawyers and Pharisees, hypocrites! You eat up the property of widows, while you say long prayers for appearance's sake' (or 'as a pretext') (Mark 12:40). Actually, this is not worship directed to the true God but to an idol: a false god created by false prophets in order to deceive themselves and the people, an invented religion which has nothing to do with the real God, the Lord of the covenant and the commandments, the God who really is. A mock obedience, offering mock consolation to the people, masquerading as worship but actually only concerned with selfish interests. Hardly any modern Marxist could be as violent in his denunciation.

God against his own work

But there is more. The Bible does not merely support the contention that religion becomes an excuse for injustice. It announces God's active purpose to overturn and destroy such idolatrous manipulations of his gifts. As a matter of fact, one of the permanent motifs in the Biblical story is God's judgment against the perverse and inhuman distortions of the signs of God's humanising mercy and righteousness. A detailed study of this Biblical tradition would be in itself a major theological task. I shall only mention four examples and suggest some consequences.

(a) In the seventh chapter of the book of Jeremiah we find the first striking paradox: Yahweh against the Temple! The Temple —and this includes also the whole ceremonial and sacrificial law—was given to Israel as a sign of the covenant. As such it was a token of God's presence, of his faithfulness and consequently of Israel's certain protection. Isaiah could exhort the people to rest assured because the house of the Lord would not be moved. But one century later Jeremiah announces: 'I will do to the house which is called by my name, and in which you trust, and to the place which I gave to you and to your fathers, as I did to Shiloh.' (Jeremiah 7:14). There is no denying that the Temple is God's gift, that he dwelt in it. But Israel is deceived when it thinks that it can ignore the law of the covenant (they deal unjustly with one another, oppress the unprotected, steal, murder, worship false gods) and at the same time take refuge in the Temple and say: 'We are delivered' (verse 10). When this happens, it is no longer God's house but 'a den of robbers'. The whole religious apparatus becomes 'an organised hypocrisy' (Skinner), which the Lord will shatter.

(b) In the gospels we meet a second paradox: Jesus against the Sabbath. Matthew 12:1–14 brings it into focus in two stories: Jesus justifies his disciples when they pluck grain to eat and he himself heals a man on the day of rest. The evangelist makes clear that Jesus answers the ensuing criticisms in the full authority of his messianic mission: 'something greater than the Temple is here', 'the Son of Man is greater than the Sabbath' (verses 6, 8). And the argument for these actions would be denounced today by many as 'horizontalist': man's needs (the disciples were hungry, the man was sick) are more important than sacred institutions for, as the prophet had said, God 'desires mercy and not sacrifice' (verse 7). In Mark's version we hear from Jesus' own lips the terse theological formulation: 'The Sabbath was made for man, not man for the Sabbath' (Mark 2:27). A legalistic and casuistic interpretation, with no regard for human need and for circumstances, had turned God's gift against man; it had imprisoned and deactivated the human significance of God's commandment. At this point, God himself intervenes – in Jesus – and breaks the Sabbath!

(c) Paul extends this paradox: faith against the Law! We cannot expect to do justice in a few lines to Paul's profound arguments and to the age-long discussion of its meaning in the Church. But the central point, as it appears in Galatians and Romans, seems very clear: the law is God's gift to his people, intended to direct them in a life according to his will, a life of active love. Sinful man has transformed the law into 'a curse', a means of

66

alienation from both God and other men. 'The works of the law'
—the formal fulfilment of prescribed actions—becomes a thing
in itself, a 'moral commodity', a kind of spiritual currency which
man can use in his transactions with God and neighbour: it
replaces trust, in relation to God, and love, in relation to man.
There is, therefore, no possibility of a right relation with God
without renouncing the alienating religion of works. God has to
restore man's right relationships 'outside the Law'.

(d) Interestingly enough, before we end our discussion of the
New Testament, we are challenged by yet another paradox in the
Letter of James: works against faith! The opposition to what Paul
had said is indeed so startling that theologians have tried all
kinds of tricks to explain it away. But it is no more striking than
the opposition between Isaiah and Jeremiah on the security of
the Temple, or between Deuteronomy and Jesus on keeping the
Sabbath. And the reason is the same: faith has also become
an excuse for inhumanity: 'If a brother or a sister is ill-clad or
in lack of daily food, and one of you says to them, "Go in peace..."
without giving them the things needed for the body ... what
does it profit? So faith by itself, if it has no works, is dead.'
(2:15 ff.). Faith is the seal of a covenant, the relationship which
God had established with his people and which has been made
perfect, fulfilled and opened to all men in Jesus Christ. When
faith is made into something separated from the whole meaning
of that covenant, when it closes on itself in a religious universe
from which man and his need—and specifically his physical,
material need—are excluded, God will not acknowledge any
more such 'faith': it will 'profit nothing'.

Certain common points in these four models deserve mention:
(i) There is no doubt in any of the models of the divine origin of
the reality under discussion: the Temple, the Sabbath, the Law,
faith are God's gracious gifts and demands; he has indeed
positively commanded man to take them with utter seriousness:
(ii) all these gifts had a purpose which was related to man's spiritual
and material welfare and fulfilment; they were not mere formal
requirements or empty gestures—they implied a total wholeness
of divine and human relationships which can be designated with
such terms as justice, faithfulness, mercy, peace; (iii) when the

gifts and commandments are separated from this purpose, when they are unhinged from God's intention, they do not merely lose all value but become *positively perverse*, they destroy man's relationship to God and to his fellow man and finally become deceptive and destroy man's own being; (iv) for this reason God has to break again and again into the life of his own people and destroy, transgress, contradict, relativise these very signs of his presence in order to restore his intention and to save man from self-deception, alienation and destruction.

Idolatry and mediation: coincidence and opposition

We have already pointed out that in all these denunciations of man's faithlessness to the covenant there is an implicit or explicit accusation of idolatry. When God's gift is separated from his purpose, when the meaning and reality of the covenant relationship are broken, then the 'god' to whom such acts and observances are directed is no longer the true Yahweh, the Lord of the covenant, but a man-made god, an image created after man's own egoistic wishes and interests. The symbol of God's care for man becomes an idol. In Israel, this is usually linked with open idolatry. But the connection is deeper and universal. In his idolatrous activity, man deceives himself doubly: on the one hand, he empties religion of its power to redeem and to restore; on the other, he creates for himself a false assurance within the circle of his unredeemed and alienated life. It is not strange that this idolatry soon becomes explicit, whether in the old worship of idols, in the religion of man or in the cult of Mammon. True faith must then express itself in prophetic iconoclasm: the denunciation and destruction of idolatrous religiosity.

In the light of these remarks, there is some justification for those Christian voices which have claimed Marx for the prophetic tradition. There is both a formal and a substantial similarity between his and the Biblical criticism of idolatry. When one makes room for the difference between philosophical/analytical and prophetic/poetic language and categories, the kinship between some of their utterances is indeed arresting. Take, for instance, these two samples:

... the worker behaves in relation to the *product of his work* as to an alien object ... The same thing happens in religion: the more man invests in God, the less he retains in himself ... The *alienation* of the worker in his product does not only mean that his work becomes an object, an *external* being, but that this being is placed *outside* him, independent of him and alien to him and that it becomes in relation to him a self-contained and substantial power, that the life which the worker has infused into the object confronts him as something alien and hostile to him ... Let us now see how we should manifest and represent in reality this concept of alienated work.

If the product of work is something alien to me and confronts me as an alien power, to whom does it belong?

To some *other* being which is not myself?

Who is this being?

The gods.[10]

Let us now read a well-known text from Isaiah:

A *man* plants a cedar and the rain makes it grow, so that later he may have cedars to cut down. It becomes fuel for his fire: some of it he takes and warms himself, some he kindles and bakes bread on it, and *some he makes into a god* and prostrates himself, shaping it into an idol and bowing down before it. The one half of it he burns in the fire ... Then, what is left of the wood he makes into a god ... and prostrates himself and prays to it, saying, 'Save me, for thou art my god!'. Such people neither know nor understand, their eyes made too blind to see, their minds too narrow to discern. Such a man *will not use his reason*, he has neither the wit nor the sense to say, 'Half of it I have burnt ... but the rest of it *I turn* into this abominable thing and so *I am worshipping a log of wood*'. He feeds on ashes indeed! *His own deluded mind* has misled him, he cannot recollect himself so far as to say, 'Why, this thing in my hand is a sham!' (Isaiah 44:14–20, NEB).

The deluded imagination, the projection of man himself into the idol, the alienation, the close connection with the economic activity of man—one is almost tempted to say: the denunciation of the fetishism of commodities—all are there.

As a first conclusion of our long exploration, we can say that Christianity and Marxism (in their original and most authentic intention) do not confront each other as respectively the defender and the accuser of religion and the gods. Christians were not unjustifiedly called 'atheists' in the Graeco-Roman world. Marxism and Christianity share the same uncompromising rejection of 'mystifications' of the product of man's activity, whether material, mental or religious. Indeed, the Bible rejects with particular violence all mystifications of God's own activity. It is concerned with 'the true God', the Lord as he himself has defined and defines his own identity in establishing his covenantal relationship—an identity in which is included the kind of human, historical life that corresponds to it. The Bible is not primarily interested in rejecting atheism but idolatry. And this is not merely a consequence of the cultural situation in which it was written, but according to the very intention of its message. The main question that it raises for man is not whether he believes or not in a deity, but to what god he is related.

A second conclusion has to do with the 'ethos' of Marx's rejection of religion. We shall not find it in the philosophical formulations, which are inherited from the Hegelian left, a heritage which Marx himself overcame in principle in his later work. We should not identify this ethos either with the militant atheism of the positivistic ideologies, although Marx—and even more clearly Engels—sometimes adopt their expressions. This is precisely a typically bourgeois ideology, and Marx specifically rejected its 'belligerent atheism' as a distracting and useless struggle. In his more mature work, religious alienation does not appear for its own sake, but as an analogy for the basic fact and reality: economic alienation. None of these things account, though, for the passion and indignation which underlie Marx's permanent rejection of religiosity in any and all forms. The secret must be found, I think, in a corresponding passion for man and his conviction that religion is the enemy of man. Whether he formulates it as the imaginary projection of man's dichotomy between his essence and his truncated existence (in the philosophical writings) or as a mystifying explanation of facts which he ought to pursue through scientific investigation, or as an ideological tool of the dominant classes and state to keep man under subjection, religion is always for him the great thief that keeps man from repossessing the powers, qualities, security that he has projected on to the gods.

This opposition is for Marx irreducible. In his Doctoral Dissertation he makes his own, in the name of philosophy, the declaration of Prometheus: 'Philosophy makes no secret of it. Prometheus' proclamation, "In a word: I hate all gods" is its own confession, its motto against all gods, in heaven or on earth, who do not recognise man's self-consciousness as the supreme divinity.'[11] Many years later, when his daughter asks him who would be his greatest example, he answers without hesitation: 'Prometheus'.[12] The driving pathos of his hatred of the gods is summed up in his passion for man. And we must concede that whoever in his time was passionately on the side of man — and particularly on the side of the oppressed and exploited proletariat — found god (in his representatives), to be on the other side. Marx could have used the bitter words of the Argentine peasant poet:

> They say that God cares for the poor:
> Well, this may be true or not,
> But I know for a fact
> That he dines with the mine-owner.

We have already noted this point and we cannot exaggerate its importance. Perhaps Girardi's statement is too sweeping when he says that 'all revolutions have clashed with Christianity, because *historically* Christianity has been structurally counter-revolutionary' and concludes: 'A revolutionary theory like Marxism was bound to be anti-Christian'.[13] But it is true enough that the churches which Marxism has encountered since its very beginning have consistently been at the service and command of the dominant classes and (with some few prophetic exceptions) deadly opposed to basic structural change. We have seen that this attitude hardly coincides with the Bible, and we shall discuss the matter again. At present, it is enough to recognise the facts.

These conclusions lead us to raise a further point: if they are true, Marx's critique of religion ought to be only 'functional', in the sense that it is at most an abstraction of the empirical evidence of how religion has functioned and functions today. As such, atheism cannot be a necessary foundation or postulate of historical materialism. But quite clearly this is not so. Marx seems to claim for his analysis of religion an almost 'metaphysical' status. Religion seems to be more for him than a historical phenomenon; it is quite literally the quintessence of alienation, the privileged expression of the ideological distortion of reality which prevents man from repossessing himself by claiming the creations of his brain and of his hands. Why is this so? A paragraph from his writing 'On the Jewish Question' seems to put us on the right track:

> The state is the mediator between man and his liberty ... It follows that, even if man declares himself to be an atheist through the mediation [*durch die Vermittlung*] of the state ... this man remains religiously captive, because he declares himself an atheist through a detour, through an intermediary [*Mittler*]. *Religion is precisely the recognition of man through a detour, through an intermediary* [*durch einen Mittler*].[14]

The rejection of all mediation seems to me to be at the very root of Marx's intellectual work. It is an effort to serve man by returning man to himself, by rejecting all attempts to erect some 'intermediate' instance. In this sense, it is absolutely wrong to see the 'proletariat' as a mediator in Marx's thinking: quite to the contrary, the role of the proletariat in the emancipation of man hinges on the fact that in this social class man's productive forces are reintegrated to the active subject. For this reason, the proletariat is the bearer of a true and final revolution.

Christianity, even in its more progressive forms, must necessarily appear as reactionary in this light, because the very heart of the Christian faith—that there is one Mediator—is the root of Marx's rejection of religion. The Christian message asserts that man can only overcome his alienation through the intervention of the true God, that he can only come to himself through God's grace. To put it briefly: in the Bible it is God who de-mystifies man; for Marx it is man who de-mystifies God. In the process, both are very suspicious and critical of religion, but from radically different perspectives. I shall later on argue the thesis that this rejection of all mediation in Marx is a result of the monistic outlook on reality which is characteristic of all German philosophy and which is, in fact, a reflection of a bourgeois mentality and the closed capitalist system. It seems to me that some of the blind spots in Marxist theory and practice are not unrelated to the inability to overcome this outlook. But we should not hasten to formulate this criticism, much less to use it as an excuse for ignoring the painful truth in what Marxism has to tell to us about ourselves as Christians.

The humorous paradox which we quoted at the beginning has a certain 'humanistic' ring: 'Thank God, that God does not exist!' In Scripture we find a serious and equally humanistic paradox: 'He [Jesus Christ] did not cling to his equality with God, but emptied himself to the condition of a slave' (Philippians 2:7, Jerusalem Bible). What is the relation between a humanistic denial of God and God's humanistic self-denial? This is a subject that we must explore further. But in any event, a Christianity which is far from shaping its life according to this model must be very careful of claiming too proudly for itself the role of spokesman and representative of God.

73

CHAPTER V

THE EXALTATION AND
THE ABOLITION OF MAN

As the cold war was raging, W. A. Visser 't Hooft, then General Secretary of the recently constituted World Council of Churches, wrote an article in which he argued that a Christian's main objection to Marxism should be directed against its practice rather than its theory, while the main criticism to Western capitalism concerned its theory rather than its practice. The idea was somewhat startling because most Christian criticism of Marxism has been almost obsessively directed against its materialism — and the ensuing mechanicalism which destroys human freedom and spirituality, its titanism — which makes an absolute of man and ends in utopianism, and its lack of a normative ethic — which results in the claim that the end justifies the means. Visser 't Hooft, on the other hand, looked at communism as a revolutionary force for justice, and complained that 'its original intention to save the masses from economic exploitation is increasingly replaced by another purpose, to maintain a rigid political system . . .'[1] The distinction between a criticism of theory and a criticism of practice is an over-simplification, because it introduces a dichotomy which is alien both to reality and to Marxism. But Visser 't Hooft was right in rejecting a purely academic discussion of the subject: Marxism confronts us, not as a mere philosophical system but as a historical movement. It claims that its theory is abstracted from reality and that it is verified in practice. Therefore, our discussion of Marxism has to be addressed both to theory and practice, and even more, to the relationship between the two. We want to devote this chapter to the exploration of some of the major issues in this area.

Such an exploration is beset with many risks. On the one hand, we must not ignore the nuances in the original formulations as well as the elaborations and corrections of the original theories which have developed in the century that has elapsed since the writings of Marx and Engels. We shall not be able to elucidate in detail the intricate theoretical problems which arise in this respect, but we shall have to recognise such questions and give them their due weight. On the other hand, it is necessary to take into account the historical conditions under which socialist revolutions have taken place and to relate them to successive theoretical formulations. In the perspective that I have taken for this study — i.e., that of a Christian committed to revolutionary change — I shall address my questions to Marxists whom I recognise as partners in a historical project, in terms of their avowed purpose to lead a liberating movement which will usher in a more human, fraternal and just society. Marxist theory and practice must be judged in relation to such purpose. In this sense, Visser 't Hooft's basic approach seems to me correct.

Marxist humanism

Is it right to pose the question in the terms we have just indicated? Does Marxism have such a programme? Can this humanistic intention be ascribed to it either on the basis of its theoretical elaboration or its historical record? To put it briefly: is Marxism — or can it be — humanist? As we know, there is today a sharp polemic within the Marxist camp on this question. I will not attempt to reproduce the involved and specialised — but by no means purely academic — arguments that have been developed in this controversy. But it seems to me that this question, which has been prompted by specific historical events, is a valid point of entry for a dialogue between Christians and Marxists concerned with human liberation.

There is little doubt that a humanist inspiration is at the origin of the Marxist movement. It is enough to read some pages of Engels's *The Condition of the Working Class in England* to realise the truth of Merleau Ponty's assertion: 'One does not become revolutionary through science but through indignation.'[2] The burning fire of moral indignation at man's inhumanity to man smoulders below the surface of even the most abstruse theoretical analyses of the early Marxists. The deep, caustic irony which runs through even the less tractable sections of *Das Kapital* points to the purpose of the author: the book is not a merely intellectual exercise or a dispassionate enquiry; it is a weapon for the proletariat in their struggle for a new society. No sensitive person can read the story of Marx, Engels, Lenin, Mao, Fidel Castro or Ché Guevara, to name only a few, without being moved by their deep compassion for human suffering and their fierce hatred of oppression and exploitation. We have already seen that Marx's hatred of the gods was—within the conditions of his experience—the obverse side of his passion for the liberation of man.

Yet no significant revolution has been born only from moral indignation and compassion: there must be a view of reality, a rationality, a revolutionary theory, a historical project, a strategy and tactics. There must also be an ideology, a total apprehension and representation of the world and of society. In his search, Marx found his first theoretical support in philosophy. 'For the young Marx,' rightly observes Althusser, ' "Man" was not only an exclamation denouncing misery and oppression. It was the theoretical principle of his conception of the world and of his practical attitude.'[3] Lenin has also pointed out German philosophy as one of the roots of Marxism. Marx inherits the tradition which, through Kant, Hegel and Feuerbach, helped him to define 'the essence of man' as his freedom and rationality socially fulfilling their total possibilities in history and rejecting all forms of religious, political and social alienation. The programme is clearly humanist: 'To be radical is to take things at the root: for man, though, the root is man himself,' he writes in 1843.[4]

The other important 'source', to use Lenin's expression, are the philosophers and activists of early French communism, from which Marx learned much of what Althusser calls 'his practical attitude'. We refer here particularly to Sismondi, Proudhon and Fourrier, and to the thinker of French industrialisation, Saint Simon. It is in contact with them that he meets the ideas of the recurrent economic crises of capitalism, of the illegitimacy of private property, of an all-transforming and imminent communist revolution. The humanist—even religious —atmosphere is here also very present.

Even as stern a critic of the idea of a Marxist humanism as Althusser is ready to admit that the humanist motivation, the idea of man's liberation, has played a significant role in all socialist movements. He ascribes to this idea an 'ideological' character, which is not for him a pejorative designation but implies a defect in relation to 'scientific' knowledge. He goes as far as saying that even an advanced communist society cannot dispense with ideology in this sense.[5] Indeed, when we observe the process of building a socialist society in China and Cuba, we see the significant, even preponderant, importance given to the creation of a new man, a solidary human being who places the common good before his own individual interest. Latin American socialist movements have given a special relevance to this theme. Guevara was thus not voicing a private opinion but the deepest ethos of the Cuban and Latin American revolutionary forces in his famous letter to the Uruguayan Journal *Marcha*:[6]

> The theory that will result [from the Cuban revolutionary process] will privilege the two pillars of the building: the formation of the new man and the development of technology ... The important question is not how many pounds of meat one can eat or how many times a year one can go to the beach, but that the individual be more fully realised, with a greater inner richness and a much greater sense of responsibility ... Let me tell you, at the risk of looking ridiculous, that a true revolutionary is led by great feelings of love.

It is true that expressions like those we have quoted do not recur in the work of 'the mature Marx'. The transition takes place around 1844–6 (the exact point of transition is strenuously debated and not without reason). Concepts like 'alienation',

77

'human essence', become less frequent and leave their place to a new vocabulary: 'social formation', 'forces of production', 'productive relations', 'structure', 'ideology'. We witness the birth of historical materialism in the strict sense of the expression. In a paragraph criticising Proudhon's 'utopianism', Marx makes clear the basic thrust of the change:[7]

> Social relations are closely bound up with productive forces. In acquiring new productive forces men change their mode of production; and in changing their mode of production, in changing their way of earning their living, they change all their social relations. The hand-mill gives you society with the feudal lord; the steam-mill, society with the industrial capitalist.

The perspective of which this passage is an apt illustration, can be sketchily summarised as follows: (1) man is not seen any more as an 'essence' to be realised, nor strictly as a moral individual; rather, we are faced with total entities called 'social formations' (feudal, capitalist, socialist, communist); (2) such social formations are not the embodiment of ideas or the result of man's planning but are determined by the 'mode of production' dominant at a given time; (3) this 'mode of production' is the basis on which the 'edifice' of a socio-economic formation rests and, in its turn, it determines (at least in principle) the character of this formation; (4) the emergence of a new mode of production is mainly dependent on the appearance of new technologies which are in turn related to new forms of ownership; (5) the basic force behind the whole process is 'need', the way in which man solves the problem of 'earning his living'; (6) the social relations that result from this situation determine in turn all superstructural elements: ideology, family, religion, culture.

This is not, of course, the whole Marx: he has not ceased to be a revolutionary in order to become a theorist of the economic process. But *he intends to give to his revolutionary project a scientific foundation and content.* What theoreticians have to to do is to understand the meaning of the struggle of the proletariat as it is taking place before their very eyes 'and to become its mouthpiece'.[8] Again, a basic outline—although very simplified—can be easily offered: (1) the industrial revolution has developed a new mode of production, industrial capitalism, for which previous relations of production (those of feudal society) are not any longer adequate; (2) there is an inbuilt irrationality in the capitalist system which leads to periodical crises due both to the increasing concentration of wealth and the relative pauperisation of the proletariat and to the fact that production, exclusively dependent on the market (lack of planning), does not correspond to need; (3) crises will escalate until a new mode of production and a consequently new social formation are reached; (4) in this critical situation, the antagonism of the social classes which results from the capitalist organisation becomes more and more violent because the oppressed class—the proletariat—cannot free itself without exploding the system as a whole.

What will be the result of this revolution? A new society in which social classes, political power—the state—and ideological thought—thought which covers rather than explains reality—will slowly disappear. In brief, the capitalist society secretes a revolutionary class, which in turn destroys this society and creates a new one. The political programme, therefore, must be to continue and to accelerate the struggle until we reach its dénouement. Meanwhile, 'the last word of social science will always be: "Le combat ou la mort".'[9]

The relationship between the different stages and articulations of the scientific-revolutionary argument could not fail to raise problems, both theoretical and practical: what is, for instance, the exact meaning of the 'determination' of consciousness by the productive process? Are ideas only a passive 'reflection' (a word which has been abused in Marxist circles but which Marx himself uses very scarcely and as a mere metaphor) of the material process? How are we to understand the 'needs' which are at the basis of the productive process, and therefore make up the driving force of history? How can the classless society be strictly a projection from the class-struggle? Is the class-struggle an element of the present capitalist social formation—destined to disappear—or is it a manifestation of the basic nature of reality, of the total material-historical process (dialectical materialism)?

If the former, how can history continue after the communist society is established? If the latter, how can we expect a classless and stateless society? The questions could be multiplied. The later work of Marx and Engels provided many elements to pursue these questions, but it also opened the possibility of different and contradictory interpretations. Such interpretations are not purely academic, hermeneutical work; they have emerged in the movement and the struggles of the socialist movements since the time of the founders and, not unfrequently, they have split the movement and unleashed violent conflicts within it. Our discussion is forced, therefore, to overflow the level of theoretical discussion and to enter into the consideration of the historical career of the socialist revolution.

The conflicts of interpretation

The Soviet revolution of 1917 was an eminently voluntaristic one. It happened in a backward society which had not yet emerged from feudalism, which had not developed large-scale industrialisation and which possessed only a small proletariat. Its triumph was very much dependent on the chaotic conditions created by the war, on an alliance between proletariat and peasants made possible partly by the war itself and on an outstanding group of revolutionary leaders originating mostly in the small nobility and the bourgeoisie. Lenin had to provide a new class analysis and Trotsky a new theory of revolution ('the permanent revolution') in order to clarify and offer theoretical support to the leap from a feudal to a socialist society. The political and economic hesitations of the early years of the revolution prove that not all theoretical problems had been rightly solved. With the advent of Stalin, the central direction soon becomes clear: the economic factor takes absolute precedence—immediate, total, galloping industrialisation. In twenty years an immense country is turned upside down and placed in conditions to withstand an enemy who was able to marshal all the resources of continental Europe. The cost of the process: absolute concentration of power, the liquidation of opposition, even within the party, the disruption of a large social group—the *kulaks*, medium and large landowners. Stalin's economicism has been stigmatised by friend and foe. The former explain it as a deviation from Marxism-Leninism, the latter as the natural outworking of its materialism. Perhaps it is more realistic and dialectical to see it as an interplay of certain subjective factors (Stalin himself, the lack of clarity and/or courage in some of the early leaders after Lenin's premature death) and objective conditions (continued conflict against European anti-Soviet aggression, the conflicting interests of the allied classes, the threat of war). Whatever the explanation, Stalinist socialism consigned all humanist hopes to the future and subordinated man (politically, culturally, morally) to the needs of economy. It dogmatised a gross materialistic psychology, it subordinated art and literature to the propaganda needs of the system (the so-called 'socialist realism') and destroyed all initiative. Stalinism has emerged as the very negation of humanism.

Over against this objectification of history, Western Marxists were reclaiming the rights of human subjectivity. The publication of Marx's early works, which began in 1932, gave to these intellectuals an inexhaustible mine of humanistic motifs and ideas. The forms that these attempts took are varied. The Frankfurt school, in particular, tried to deepen the understanding of dialectics by penetrating the processes of consciousness. How is man's creativity related to the actual material conditions but also able to project them utopically and thus to conceive the hope that is the dynamic force behind history? (Bloch). Should not 'human needs' include also 'spiritual needs' such as self-affirmation, the need of losing oneself among others, aggressiveness? (Horkheimer). Do we not find in Marx a conception of the totality of history and therefore a dialectics of man's self-creation as the inner meaning of history? (Adorno). How does class-consciousness really emerge, to be sure in relation to objective conditions, but not merely as a reflection of them? (Lukacs). Is it not necessary to relate Marx's understanding of the aliena-tion created by capitalist society to Freud's analysis of the mechanisms of that alienation as it operates in the subconscious and thus to uncover the repressive character of our whole civilisa-tion (including the Soviet society)? (Marcuse).[10]

In Italy, in a polemic conversation with the idealist philosopher of history Benedetto Croce, the communist leader and martyr Gramsci was also searching for a view of proletarian consciousness that would overcome Stalinist mechanicalism. Marxism is for him primarily a revolutionary theory, a world-view concerned with the movement of history. Correspondingly, he creates a Communist Party which leaves the philosophical question (dialectical materialism) as optional but rests on the common commitment to revolutionary action, an act of will which is not arbitrary but rational, i.e. corresponding to objective historical needs (historical materialism). Later on, when Stalin's star fell and the gates of criticism were opened, a humanist spring swept over Marxism. Economic analysis found again its place in the perspective of the humanist programme of the early Marx. On the basis of their common concern for man, Christians and Marxists began to move, in Europe, 'from anathema to dialogue'.

The French Marxist philosopher and at one time secretary of the Communist Party in his country, Louis Althusser, seems to have been the first to challenge, from a rigorous theoretical point of view, this new humanist interpretation. We need not go into much detail. 'Humanism' is for him an ideological approach to reality, which corresponds to the earlier stages of Marx's thought, before he had pierced through to a scientific understanding of history. Ideology is the way in which man 'lives' his relations and his world; science uncovers the real relations. As we have seen, Althusser thinks that this dichotomy cannot be totally overcome and that the dialectics of the 'experienced' and the (theoretically) 'known' relations of man with his world will continue to exist even in a communist society. Yet, in historical and dialectical materialism, Marx offers—according to Althusser—a total theory through which this 'humanist vision' is exposed in its ideological character and related to the real conditions and relations in which it emerges. In such a theory, the ideological concepts of 'human subject' and 'human essence' are replaced by an understanding of '. . . the different specific *levels* of *human praxis* (economic, political, ideological, scientific action) in their characteristic articulations, based on the specific articulations in the unity of a human society'.[11] In other words, the real object is 'a social formation', a definite structure, and the individual is, to use a figure, only a point of encounter and interaction of the force-lines of the total magnetic field. In order to know man, therefore, one must 'reduce to ashes the philosophical [ideological] myth of man'.[12] In this sense, Althusser speaks of 'a theoretical anti-humanism of Marx'.[13]

Althusser's arguments have evoked different reactions. Some Christians have received them gladly. They seem to make a sharp distinction between science and ideology—in the larger and possibly positive sense which Althusser gives to it—and, by restricting Marxism to the former, they leave the possibility of holding to faith within the 'lived' and 'subjective' area of ideology. Yet it seems to me that, while the distinction between science and faith is a necessary one, Althusser's view in which the two are simply two ways of grasping the same subject, i.e. the reality of a social formation, and in which science constitutes the *knowing* and therefore the superior and definite way, cannot be accepted from a Christian point of view. From another angle, Althusser's structuralism has been severely criticised for ignoring the movement of history. Reality is for him a structure of relationships, which can be theoretically codified. The possibility of the emergence of something genuinely new, of real history, seems negated from the start. Change can only be a relatively new reorganisation of the elements within an already established structure of relationships. Was this really what Marx and Engels intended? Is this still a revolutionary theory? Several authors have pointed out that, in effect, Althusser's 'domination' of Marxist thought in France for several years has produced a certain sterility in both theoretical and practical research. Some Latin Americans have asked whether this 'structuralist' reading of Marx cannot be suspected of being, after all, an 'ideological' justification of the accommodation of the French Communist Party to the *status quo* and of its revolutionary impotence!

In the aftermath of such heated polemics, some new possibilities are emerging of a 'Marxist humanism' that heeds Althusser's powerful warning against losing 'Marx's most precious gift to the world: the possibility of scientific knowledge'[14] without at the same time dissolving the human subject into a mere knot of relationships and history into a synchronic structure. I refer particularly to the work of such Marxists as the Frenchman Lucien Sève and the German Helmut Fleischer, who have deepened such categories as 'need' and 'conditioning' and found, without resorting to an idealist perspective, the place and meaning of human subjectivity and freedom. I find these expressions of Marxist thought very significant for a rethinking of Christian ethics, so frequently cast in idealistic and subjective individualistic categories. To this we shall return in the last chapters.[15]

Searching for a perspective

This complex—and nevertheless over-simplified—discussion of the 'history' of Marxist humanism seems to me necessary in order to find a right perspective for our problem. The variety and conflict of interpretations seems to me to arise from a wrong approach to the many-sided phenomenon which we call Marxism, i.e. a view which takes it to be a self-enclosed and self-sufficient entity, a set of theoretical tenets once for all formulated by Marx and Engels and afterwards more or less faithfully interpreted and practised by their followers. In contrast to this, I want to submit a different—and I think more historical interpretation. In my view, one should set Marxism in the context of the long heritage of man's aspirations and struggles for a more human and just organisation of individual and social life. These struggles, always partly successful and partly frustrated, combine moral aspirations, the possibilities and conditionings afforded by scientific and technological progress and man's intellectual effort to penetrate and take control of the dynamics of human history and social relationships. The movement reaches a new qualitative level with the extraordinary and rapid technological and scientific developments of the modern age. Lenin is quite right in discerning the main currents which, at the time of Marx, sum up and bring to fruition some of man's more promising efforts: German philosophy as the attempt to understand the movement of history, the way in which thought and reality interact and determine each other; the research of the English economists to discover the laws of man's work and transactions, the secrets of the industrial capitalist world which exploded all hitherto established forms of dealing with wealth and work relations, and the moral passion of the French utopian socialists, trying to bring to fruition a new organisation of society in which the possibilities offered by the industrial world would be liberated from their captivity to a structure of privilege and exploitation and made available to all men in conditions of justice and equality.

In order to integrate into a single theoretical political perspective this manifold heritage, Marx is forced to assimilate and to overcome it. This is the connecting thread of his own biography. He explores Hegelianism from within and discovers its significance and its essential failure: it is necessary to turn it upside down (which is in fact to put it on its feet), to bring it down from the abstract realm of the Idea, in which it could only lead to the intellectual justification of the *status quo*, and to root it in reality, in the realm of the material and social world. He participates in the struggles of the proletariat with its moral earnestness, but discovers its crippling weakness: it is necessary to rescue it from a voluntaristic world of imperatives and to anchor it firmly in the actual conditions of the economic reality which offers the only possibility of a real transformation. He penetrates the dynamics of economic development which the economists had laid bare, but rejects their unconscious functionalist frame of reference by connecting them with the real conditions of existence of the working class. Thus, he possesses the heritage in the only possible way: by transforming it. The transformation is so radical and wide-ranging that it has given to many the impression of a total negation. Hence, this illusion of a self-sufficient and self-contained entity which has misled so many interpreters and followers, who want to find in Marx himself the answer to all the questions and the origin of all socialism.

The truth is that, while challenging and overcoming his heritage, Marx also offers a future to it. Or, which is more important, he offers a future to the social revolutionary movements of which this heritage was both expression and impulse. It does so by providing a set of analytic tools and a revolutionary theory. In this sense, Althusser and others are right in insisting that Marx's contribution must be judged by his mature scientific thought. But it is also true that, by gathering up this past, Marxism as a movement has inherited the utopian vision, the humanist passion, the concern for a total view of reality which was inherent in these traditions. A 'chemically pure' Marxism does not exist—and if it existed it is doubtful that it would have any interest. *Marxism does not stand by itself.* A genuine assessment of the socialist movement in its totality and significance for our society must neither underestimate the original and decisive contribution of Marxism nor ignore the persistence and importance of this previous tradition and subsequent experience. Thus, the history of the socialist movement is part of the interpretation of Marxism.

CHAPTER VI

TOWARDS AN ETHICAL
EVALUATION OF MARXISM

THE PERSPECTIVE ELABORATED in the last chapter would
indicate that it is not arbitrary to subject Marxism to an ethical
evaluation. Nevertheless, it is necessary to sound at least two
warnings before attempting it. The first is that we cannot proceed
on the basis of an idealist ethics which begins with abstract
notions like freedom, truth or goodness. Rather, we must ask
about the validation of the Marxist claim to offer a revolutionary
theory based on scientific analysis as an efficient tool for the
historical mission of the proletariat of destroying the unjust and
inadequate capitalist system and ushering in a new historical
age. What can be said about Marxism as a revolutionary movement after one century? In the second place, those of us from the
West, and particularly Christians, should be careful before
indulging in self-righteous denunciation of 'Stalinist terror' and
'communist oppression' without realising that at least as much
terror and oppression—often even without hope—is abroad in
the Western world under the pretence of defending 'Christian
values' and 'the Christian way of life'. Nothing that a 'horrified'
European bourgeois can read about Soviet terror in Solzhenitsyn's
Gulag Archipelago is new to the subjects of the 'most Christian'
governments of Brazil, Uruguay or Chile!

The socialist record

As Christians, we have not a set of abstract values, but a very concrete number of prophetic criteria: justice to the poor and oppressed, protection of the weak, attention to those who suffer hunger, freedom to slaves and the oppressed. When we look at the history of socialist movements in this light, some facts acquire a theological significance. While Asia continues to be visited by the apocalyptic horseman called hunger, communist China has practically eliminated malnutrition, illiteracy and premature mortality for 800 million people in less than thirty years. While the Caribbean countries, constantly 'helped' by the USA, continue to stumble from economic crisis to economic crisis, frequently in the grip of terror, instability and inflation, the island of Cuba, subjected to economic blockade, has been able to develop in less than twenty years the basis for prosperous agriculture and cattle raising, has established universal education and is beginning to develop new forms of political participation of the people in public life. Even Soviet Russia, beset by military aggression during the first five years of the revolution and having to cope with the full weight of Hitler's aggression on a three-thousand-mile front during World War II, has moved from a feudal, backward society into a modern industrial nation in half a century. The data could be multiplied: Marxist socialism can claim indeed to have proved a powerful and efficient motor of social change, economic development and scientific progress.

We must also record the human cost of these achievements: the liquidation of certain social groups, the restrictions to liberty (while we must remember that 'liberal freedoms' have little reality for economically, intellectually and even biologically submerged masses), the arbitrary exercise of power, the disruption of religious and family traditions which often give meaning and hope to the life of 'the little in the land'. But this cost must be balanced off against the price paid, for instance, by the British proletariat for the Industrial Revolution (so well portrayed in nineteenth-century literature), or the human cost of Western development for Africa, Asia and Latin America. Again, when looking at the more humane conditions of work which have appeared in the Western countries, one must realise to what extent they are the result of the constant struggle, fertilised by the blood of so many martyrs, of a proletariat which found in Marxism both a theory, an ideology and a courageous leadership. Whatever our misgivings, it is difficult not to feel a sense of admiration and gratitude for a movement that, in less than a century, through its direct action in some areas and through indirect influence in labour movements and other social forces in others, has raised to a human condition the life of at least half of the human race!

Yet the present situation of Marxism does not correspond to its revolutionary heritage. Perhaps the most important fact in the world situation of today is the deterioration of the historical Marxist movement in terms of its revolutionary potential. The country with the longest 'socialist history', the USSR, leaves a very painful impression. It is not only — and perhaps not mainly — the absence of some forms of liberty after more than half a century. The most serious sign is the apparent inability to move in the direction of a real communist society: a society in which each one would contribute according to his ability and be rewarded according to his needs, in which the administration of things would replace the government of men — the state would slowly disappear — the society without social classes, free from constraint. On the basis of a purely economicist criterion, the Communist Party of the USSR declared that the Union had fulfilled the socialist stage and was moving towards a communist society. But this sounds as a rather hypocritical and ideological declaration when we see this society assuming a number of the characteristics of capitalism: a market economy, material private incentives, a system of enterprise administration. Moreover, the Third World becomes more and more cynical regarding the socialist countries' solidarity in our struggle for liberation when these countries become increasingly integrated economically with the multinational capitalist corporations (which they so vociferously denounce!), when they vote with Western imperialist powers in the UNCTAD or FAO meetings against fair terms of trade for the Third World, when the Communist Parties directed from Moscow seem much more concerned with a pacific co-existence favourable to the USSR than with the revolutionary change needed in the Third World. USSR policy seems to follow the instruction that a Latin American president is said to have given to his chauffeur: 'Signal left and turn right!'

The political and economic quality and the human value of socialist revolutions has consistently increased as we move from USSR to China and Cuba. The social cost has been reduced, the measure of compulsion and repression, particularly in the last case, has been minimised, the welfare of the people has been given at least as much priority as economic development, the disruptive consequences of a blind drive towards industrialisation have been avoided. The Chinese and Cuban revolutions have created a sense of participation and achievement on the part of the people and have stimulated a feeling of dignity and moral determination. Although one-party rule, with its unavoidable injustices and impoverishment of participation and its tendency towards bureaucratisation was still fully enforced, the extraordinary leadership of Mao and Fidel has opened the way for a dynamism and renewal which were totally absent in the USSR after the first two or three years. But the internal advantages of the Chinese revolution contrast with its relative lack of interest in the struggle of the countries of the Third World. Moreover, the conflict between the USSR and China has weakened the socialist camp and introduced a number of rifts and divisions in the liberation movements in the Third World. The atomisation of the left is one of the most painful facts of the present situation.

The picture is not much more encouraging when one looks at the communist-led powerful trade-unions in the West. The proletariat of the industrialised countries, in which Marx saw the agent of revolution, seem to have no sense of revolutionary vocation but rather to have been totally integrated into the capitalist system, and their leaders are much more interested in obtaining immediate economic vindications within the framework of the national situation than in the world-wide solidarity of the proletariat sung in the 'International' or declared in the 'Communist Manifesto'. The workers of the nineteenth century had 'nothing to lose but their chains'. Now, they stand to lose more and consequently tend to forget their unity ... even with the foreign workers who suffer in their midst!

A realistic evaluation of the overall present situation seems to show that the need for a socialist revolution on world scale is today more urgent than ever. It is so for the mere survival of mankind, threatened to death by the blind forces of destruction, waste, exploitation and oppression unleashed by the capitalist system in its global expansion. Yet precisely now, the traditional Marxist movement suffers from a severe crisis and an almost total loss of revolutionary power, efficiency and even will. One would dare to say that, if Marxism has still a historical task to fulfil, it must undergo a deep renewal, it must receive a new historical impulse and find new form of expression and new channels of action. This may sound startling and even reactionary to some Marxists who seem to take for granted their revolutionary credentials. But, as a whole, Western Marxist countries and parties are rapidly losing their credibility in the Third World and their flags are taken up by movements which are ready to revise theory and practice in terms of an effective revolutionary change and the construction of a genuine socialism.

The permanent validity of Marxism

If the rather hard judgment which we have expressed is true, why bother still about Marxism? Should we not say that it has run its course? In a certain sense, this is true. Our thesis is that the Marxist movement has, to a large extent, lost its ethos and is, at the present time, unable to provide the stimulus for revolution and to steel the masses to active engagement in the struggle for a socialist society of global dimensions. On the other hand, no revolutionary movement can exempt itself from Marxist analysis and ideology. This is precisely the meaning of the experience of the 'third ways' in their Christian democratic or 'populist' forms: their lack of consistent analysis and ideology finally delivers them at the doorstep of capitalism. What is, therefore, to be found in Marxism of permanent and indispensable significance for a revolutionary movement? Why can we not return to a utopian or idealist socialism which perhaps would pose fewer problems for Christians? I think that we have to refer here to four inter-related elements. This is what I concretely mean by the 'Marxism' which is a permanent core of any struggle for liberation.

1. The first element is the understanding of history as ultimately dependent on man's organisation of the process through which he produces the goods to satisfy his needs. We need not take this affirmation in the sense that economic activity unilaterally and exclusively determines all human life. Man is no mere *homo faber*, nor is the relation between so-called 'infrastructure' and 'super-structure' a one-way street. The main point here is that history is not primarily the unfolding of man's consciousness or of his ideas but the dynamics of his concrete activity, the main form of which is the work through which he transforms nature in order to respond to the totality of his needs. This idea can, to be sure, be misinterpreted in a narrow sense as limiting history to man's effort to find food and shelter, but it need not be so if 'need' is seen in terms of man's total experience.

2. The second element is the recognition that 'man' is not the single individual but a communal unity in the form of a concrete social formation with its structures, relationships and self-understanding (ideology). Some may read this affirmation as a negation of personhood. But it need not be so understood; what it means, is, at least, that society is not an aggregate of autonomous individuals but that the primary fact is a totality and that the individual can only be reached—indeed he can only emerge—within the network of relationships which form his existence.

3. Thirdly, there is the fact of class struggle and the revolution-ary role of the proletariat. I think that we must take this affirma-tion in a very specific sense as referring to the social formation in which we live, the capitalist industrial world: 'An oppressed class is the vital condition for every society founded on the antagonism of classes. The emanicaption of the oppressed class thus necessarily implies the creation of a new society.'[1] Class struggle is for Marx first of all a fact; it is the dynamics created by a system of production in which economic power (possession of the means of production) is concentrated in an increasingly reduced number of people while the growing majority are forced to sell their labour force—which actually means their basic human

92

activity. The inadequacy of such a situation becomes increasingly clear and the need to redress it will objectively lead the oppressed to destroy the form of property which shapes this society and to create a new form of organising work, production and distribution (a socialist society) and the forms of consciousness and political organisation corresponding to it. The fact that capitalism was able to 'buy off' its proletariat in the developed world through the use of the 'external proletariat' of the Third World has disguised class-struggle and led many in the West to deny its existence. But a look at the total scene tends to confirm Marx's view. It is possible to differ as to the political course that must be taken; it is certainly necessary to review in many respects Marx's own class analysis; it is possible that the bearer of the revolution may not be the industrial proletariat as Marx envisaged it. But it would be illusory — and therefore reactionary — to expect basic structural changes except through the struggle of those who suffer from the present organisation of society. The struggle of 'the poor', not as an isolated and haphazard phenomenon, but in their organic and structural existence as oppressed classes and peoples is the only indispensable and certain force for change. The future of mankind is, in historical terms, dependent on this struggle.

4. This leads to a final point: the notion of praxis. This is today a very debated subject within Marxism. It must be clear that it does not mean that man can undertake an arbitrary or purely voluntaristic transformation of the world. But it means, at least, that true knowledge can only be acquired starting from the concrete actions of men, that theory has meaning only as it leads to a course of action which proves significant and that action itself becomes the test of theory. Truth is not found in the contemplation of a Platonic world of ideas or in the exploration of subjective consciousness but in the scientific analysis of the activity of human beings within the conditions of their social situation. Knowledge finds its place as an activity as it reacts back on that situation, correcting our activity in the sense of its objective conditions. Revolutionary action is not an intrusion in the world: it is a response to reality and, in turn, it moves the world towards its realisation. Philosophy is thus not concerned

any more with merely 'explaining the world'; it aims at 'transforming it'. Perhaps one should say: the only way to explain the world is to transform it.

An anti-Christian philosophy?

Christians have found difficulty in all the points we have mentioned as the 'indispensable Marxist contribution' to revolutionary change. These seem to contradict the Christian view of God, of the world, of ethics. This discussion will occupy us for the rest of this book. We shall now merely open it by asking whether these four Marxist tenets, as we have defined them, do in fact run counter to the Christian faith. Christianity does not offer a philosophy, just as it does not offer a particular political or social system. But this does not mean that it has no questions in these areas, arising from its own particular insight as shaped by what it claims to be God's own revelation of his purpose and will. On this basis, it is led sometimes to reject a philosophy or a social programme. Is this the case in relation to these Marxist elements?

It has been taken for granted that Christianity stands opposed to Marxism on account of the latter's materialism. On the other hand, several theologians have called attention to what William Temple described as 'the materialism of the Christian faith'. Things become a little clearer when we realise that 'materialism' is not in Marx opposed to the 'spiritual' dimension in human life, but to the 'idealistic' understanding of man and history. The problem has become complex and clouded because, in their rejection of idealism, Marx and even more Engels, borrowed much of the language and even philosophy of the eighteenth- and nineteenth-century humanist and positivistic materialists, and this confusion between positivistic and 'dialectical' materialism was even reinforced in the official line of the Communist Parties. Moreover, there is a deeper sense in which a Christian will challenge, not so much Marx's materialism as the total philosophical heritage which he transforms but does not question radically enough.

In spite of these reservations, it is my conviction that Christian theology — and particularly one which tries to be evangelical — has no business in defending an idealist outlook and can only confuse things by remaining captive to a philosophy which is extraneous to the Biblical perspective and has been introduced into Christianity through the acute process of Hellenisation which historians of doctrine since Harnack have so well documented. Several points must be made in this respect. The Bible is undoubtedly emphatic about the possibility and the reality of man's moral and spiritual relationship with his neighbour and with God. But such a relationship is never conceived in an 'idealist' way but clearly mediated through material, historical events and realities. This is the reason why mystics have always found difficulty with the interpretation of the Bible and were forced to read it 'metaphorically' or 'allegorically' as a somewhat condescending 'material way' of conveying 'spiritual realities' which were open only to the initiated. But, quite to the contrary, the world of matter is in the Scriptures neither an illusion nor the shadowy and despicable projection of ideas and consciousness but God's good creation and the realm of his action. God's covenants with man — whether in creation, after the flood, in Sinai or the 'New Covenant' in Christ, always involves 'worldly' relationships: man is placed as responsible for creation; he is given a law dealing with the material and the social world; he is called to see 'God in the flesh' — what our eyes have seen and our hands touched! At the centre of our faith there is an unavoidable physical and historical reality: cross, resurrection, the sacraments, the resurrection of the body, a new heaven and a new earth. Idealism — the attempt to dissolve these realities into subjective feelings, ideas or symbols — is in Christian terms a heresy, whether it comes in the guise of neoplatonic gnosticism, spiritualistic mysticism, subjective pietism or liberal Hegelian, Kantian or existentialist philosophy! Our discussion with Marxist materialism cannot be engaged at this point. We must take for granted the reality and uppermost significance of the material world and the material basis of human relationships and social processes.

Individualistic conceptions of man are no less anti-Biblical. Neither sin nor salvation are in the Bible put in such a framework:

the former is a condition of mankind, our humanity as it is 'in Adam', in the old realm of decay and death in which the whole creation is alienated and perverted—and groans for its release and redemption. Salvation is man's participation by faith and love into the new realm opened by the death and resurrection of Jesus Christ—the new life that moves towards its consummation in the 'new world', God's new creation. Precisely this fact that individual man is not seen as an autonomous reality, able to extricate himself from this 'common humanity' which shares in the solidarity of sin and redemption, has been a stumbling block for liberal theology. 'Free will,' a neutral man who can decide and manage his life on the basis of his moral and intellectual efforts, has been from the time of Pelagius a recurrent heresy. Liberal theology has made great efforts to 'excuse' the Bible from this scandalous collectivism by attributing it to a defective psychology or sociology.

We may ask how is it possible, on the basis of this common solidary humanity, to direct to man's consciousness the powerful call to repentance and conversion that sounds throughout the Bible. A similar question has been addressed to Marxism: how is it possible to invite to revolution a man who is collectively determined by his material relations. The logical dilemma is posed in both cases by the profound insight into the depth of human alienation and the unbreakable solidarity of mankind. And the answer is found in both cases, not in a clever intellectual argument but in the answer to the liberating message itself, in the praxis of engagement. The deep-going difference between the two lies in the ultimate ground of the freedom which enables man to listen to this call. Christianity has no reason to defend the bourgeois concept of an autonomous individual!

We will discuss the character of Marxist and Christian ethics in the next chapters. But it is important to point out from the beginning that there are no abstract ethics in Scripture. Love, justice or freedom are never extolled or required as general values or ideal norms but always embodied in concrete relationships: it is justice to the poor, the orphan, the widow, the foreigner; it is love for a specific neighbour, or a specific enemy, freedom from a particular slavery: political, economic, or from the curse of the law, or from the captivity of death. The Kantian 'moral imperative' as a purely formal obligation, or 'humanity' as a general content of it are totally foreign to Biblical thinking. It is very interesting to note that, even when Stoic ethics are incorporated by Paul in his ethical teaching (for instance in Colossians 3 or Ephesians 4), it is immediately related and made concrete by references to particular relationships and circumstances within the life of the community.

The point of divergence

In so far, then, as historical or even dialectical materialism would limit itself to asserting that human life must be seen as the history of man's involvement in the domination and transformation of the world (work), as the effort to respond to human needs, in the context of a net of interconnecting relationships which embraces the whole of society, the Christian faith need not feel scandalised or threatened by such a theory. In so far, also, as Marxism says, that man's coming to himself takes place within and in terms of these relationships, there is also nothing to object. (To be sure, the particular account of these relationships – the socio-economic analysis – given in Marxism must be critically examined in terms of its pertinence and accuracy: this is not a theological but a scientific issue and must be solved as such).

But historical and dialectical materialism does not stop here: it presents itself as a total, all-embracing, self-sufficient and exclusive understanding of reality; as exhaustive and absolute and therefore ruling out all reality and relationships outside its purview. In so doing it flatly contradicts the Christian faith and raises for itself problems which seem to me unsolvable, as the very history of Marxism indicates.

If the reality of evil, or alienation, or their concrete forms as class oppression, the fetishism of commodities or money, can be exhaustively traced back to an inadequate arrangement of the economic process, or perhaps more specifically to private property of the means of production, how is the origin of such maladjustment to be explained or understood? Even more important: how can the persistence of these things be explained

D   97

and overcome when private property has been eliminated as in socialist countries? How can socialist societies 'miss the way'? Why is it that alienation of work, of human freedom, find new expressions — bureaucracy, the 'new class', the 'cult of personality' — in the socialist state? In other words, it would seem that the Marxist view of the human problem is insufficient — and to that extent misleading — because it does not take seriously enough the depth of man's alienation and consequently of the problems of power, of man's self-interest, of the intractability of human relationships.

The problem can be put in other terms. Let us grant that we cannot pose the existence of abstract values or moral laws. 'The good', in human terms, is the realisation of the possibilities that emerge in concrete conditions. The measure of what is 'human' or 'inhuman' at a given time depends on the economic, techno-logical, psychological conditions obtaining at that point in history. We cannot judge abstractly the facts of slavery, feudalism or, let us say, human rights. But questions are more complex than that: which of the several possibilities for technological progress should be pursued? How are we to adjudge the balance between the fulfilment of minimum possibilities for today or for certain sectors of mankind and the needs and possibilities of future generations? Problems are endless in this respect. Some Marxist theorists have tried — as we have seen — to develop a 'humanist' criterion based on the work of the earlier Marx; others have tried to refine the concept of 'need' by analysing the interplay of basic, material needs and elaborate spiritual needs. But in both cases the question as to the direction in which a progressive self-realisation of man in society is to be pursued is far from solved. This is no mere theoretical question: the important divergence between China's, Cuba's and the USSR's goals for their planning indicates the presence of hidden or avowed different understandings of the realisation of humanity. One would have to mention also the more 'heterodox' socialisms of Yugoslavia or Tanzania to see the scope of the question. The problem of ethics cannot be solved by Lenin's clever dictum that 'the good is that which is good for the proletariat' because what is good for the proletariat is by no means self-evident — at least once we move beyond a basic minimum!

Still another aspect of the question relates to the hope for the future. Marx does not abound—and this is to his credit—in elaborate descriptions of the classless society which the socialist revolution will eventually usher in. But the few somewhat symbolic descriptions and the whole ethos of the communist movement suggests the importance of this element of hope, of this utopian dimension. But how is the dialectics of progress to be understood once class struggle has ended and therefore the basic contradiction has been removed? We are usually told that contradictions will never be totally eliminated from human existence, and therefore history will continue: but how are we to understand the nature of these contradictions? Are they merely related to the struggle to dominate nature? Is a philosophy of automatic progress the ground for Marxist historical optimism? This would be a most shaky foundation, particularly for a materialist philosophy. After all, the belief in progress is a peculiarly idealist product and when materialism tries to incorporate it into itself, it is involved in very serious contradictions. Thus, it is not surprising that Engels, who tries this way in his 'dialectics of nature', ends up in the rather gloomy philosophy of an eternal return!

These questions are not meant in a self-righteous or apologetic spirit. They are frequently used as pretexts for the defence of the *status quo*. Certainly capitalism has no answer to them: its hypocritical lip-service to spiritual realities, to ideas, to progress and freedom hardly disguises its crass, total materialism in the most degrading sense of the word. Nor can Christians parade their answers to these questions as long as their practice does not show their historical relevance. These problems are posed, therefore, not in order to reject or invalidate the revolutionary strength and impulse of Marxism but in real earnest lest the revolutionary potential and crucial importance of the Marxist contribution be threatened by its refusal to face squarely some of these problems.

If I understand it correctly, the ethos of the whole Marxist attempt can be encapsulated in one affirmation: solidarity (love?) is better than egoism. Explain the 'better' in any terms; this is Marxist humanism. I am aware that this summary affirmation will be dismissed by many, Marxists and anti-Marxists, as naïve, capricious or superficial. I am convinced, nevertheless, that it can be established and validated through a careful study of the mainstream of Marxist revolutionary thinking beginning with Marx himself. It presupposes that, as the French Marxist Maximilien Rubel has argued,[2] Marx's theoretical work finds its focus within an ethos rooted in the humanist tradition. It further claims that, for all the rhetoric against love, the rejection of capitalist egoism and individualistic self-seeking is the core of Marx's ethics. Solidarity is the positive expression of this rejection. It comes to clear and direct expression in a paragraph from Lenin:

> The old society was based on the following principle: either you loot your neighbour or he loots you; either you work for somebody else or somebody works for you: you are either a slave or a slave-owner. And it is understandable that men, educated in such a society, will assimilate, together with their mother's milk, as it were, the psychology, the habits, the idea that there is nothing but master or slave, or small owner or small employee, officer or intellectual, in one word, *men who are exclusively engaged in caring for themselves and what is theirs, without thinking of others.* [Revolution] is a victory over our own routine and weakness, *over petit bourgeois egoism,* over all those habits which an accursed capitalism has left as a heritage to the worker and peasant.[3]

We seem to hear the announcement of Guevara's terse sentence: 'a revolutionary is a person possessed by deep feelings of love'.

But it seems to me that this basic ethos is not only unjustified but excluded by the philosophical framework which Marxism has chosen. Neither a self-contained materialism nor a self-contained idealism can really say that 'solidarity is better than egoism'. As a matter of fact, both idealism and the materialism which emerges as its counterpart are totalising systems which attempt to subsume all reality under a single and univocal notion, which can be dominated in thought and action and placed at one's service. Historically, it is possible to see these systems as the philosophical expression of the European ethos of conquest and domination, which is unable to 'respect' any other reality—whether a nation, a race, a culture—but can only relate to it by appropriating, dominating and subjecting it to slavery. Hegel has given to this ethos a most illuminating expression in his dialectics of the master and the slave. According to it, the self reaches its realisation only through the appropriation of the other or the rebellion in which the master is denied. But it is not enough to turn this dialectics upside down in order to exorcise its ethos. There is in it no place for solidarity, because solidarity is based on differentiation, on the existence of a real 'other' whom I do not absorb into myself or use instrumentally for my own self-realisation. We are not dealing here with merely theoretical propositions; what is at stake is the possibility of real liberation, whether we face the relation of man and woman, education, or the developed countries' relation to the Third World. It is no matter of chance that this 'dialectical monism' begins to be challenged from the areas of the world in which the experience of dependence and domination has opened the eyes to the need of not merely reversing oppression, but opening the possibility of real solidarity in the recognition of 'the other'.[4]

Dialectical materialism as usually understood, as a self-contained system, does not offer a place for any 'exteriority', for anything that genuinely remains outside its power, for anything which claims a freedom which I can neither give nor take away, in short, for a real 'other'. In Christian terms we would say that the ultimate and original ground of this self-containment is the denial of the 'other', the attempt to incorporate even God into our own self, to make him a function of man. If I understand it correctly, this is the *bourgeois* spirit (is it not significant that liberal theology, the theology of the bourgeoisie, has been consistently reductionistic?). This is real atheism: God is denied in the neighbour and the neighbour in God. Marx struggled to break society open, to destroy bourgeois solipsism and egoism. But it seems to me that he retained the philosophy of identity, of self-containment, which is the objectification of this bourgeois spirit. What one would like to invite our Marxist partners to do is not to become Christians—this belongs, indeed, in another context—but to take seriously the question as to how can solidarity be really motivated and widened unless there is, at every level of thought and action, the real possibility of openness to 'the other'.[5]

We are not proffering a charge against Marx; it is rather a charge against ourselves as Christians. Against a god who absorbed man into himself, Marx retorted by absorbing god into mankind. In the 1844 Manuscripts, Marx speaks of 'the privileged and idle possessors'. This bourgeois god who is 'a privileged and idle possessor' writ large, Marx rejected with repugnance and passion. But this is not the real God. The God of the covenant, the God of Jesus Christ is the servant and solidary one, the God who exists in solidarity and for solidarity, the 'faithful one' as the Scripture calls him. It is the God whom one cannot affirm without affirming man, because he has declared himself on the side of man forever, and has sealed this affirmation with his own life. But how can a comfortable bourgeois Christianity, made up of happy possessors, allied with every form of oppression and exploitation, name such a God?

CHAPTER VII

GOD IN HEAVEN AND
GOD IN HISTORY

MARX'S PREFERENCE FOR Prometheus has two sides. Prometheus symbolises rebellion — he dares to defy the gods. But he also
symbolises solidarity — he incurs the wrath of the gods in order
to help man. The movement of Marx's thought seems to be
impelled by the wish to find in the very heart of reality (finally
the economic process) that power of transformation and humanisation that mankind had located in the gods. Very early in his
life he had written to his father: 'If the gods had before dwelt
above the earth, they have now become its centre.'[1] Prometheus,
human affirmation — rebellion and solidarity — at the centre of
history: this seems to me the pulsing heart of Marxism as a
historical movement.

Both Marx and Engels write caustically against Christian love.
Their anger and cynicism are quite understandable when one
looks at the use to which Christian love has been put — both by
naïve Christians and by cunning 'fellow travellers' of Christianity.
But it seems to me that it is precisely at this point where we find
the language in which we can — as Christians — articulate our
revolutionary intention in such a way that it may become
understandable — though not necessarily acceptable — to our
Marxist friends. I shall therefore try now to gather up the
theological fragments which we have examined previously and
put them within a total theological perspective under the over-
arching Biblical conception of love. Three brief preliminary
remarks may be in order:

(a) My intention in doing this is not apologetic, in the sense of trying to force an argument that will convince any reasonable person that the Christian faith is 'better' than Marxism as a world-view. I am not interested in 'cornering' the Marxist in order to 'force' him to recognise an intellectual or moral superiority of Christianity. The Christian Gospel does not enter the 'ideological market' as a product. It simply and soberly gives an account of its hope. For the Christian, faith does not come at the end of a clever argument. Faith witnesses to the truth that it has grasped, or rather by which it has been grasped—and rests in the power to convince of God's own Spirit.

(b) I am not trying to establish coincidences, to strike an ideological bargain, least of all to accommodate the Gospel to Marxism. The Christian faith has its own rationality, in terms of its own horizon. It does not therefore shrink from making the bold claims that sound scandalous. This is the only attitude that is worthy of a faithful relationship. Guevara himself, in calling Christians to claim and honour their revolutionary inheritance, insisted that they should not 'have the cowardice to hide their convictions in order to assimilate themselves to the Marxists'. Christians and Marxists, engaged in a concrete human project and action, have the responsibility of holding faithfully to their own and to examine honestly each other's deepest commitments and convictions, honouring them in courageous action as well as in outspoken and explicit expression.

(c) Therefore, I have to ask the Marxist—or agnostic—friends who have followed us so far, to have the seriousness and patience necessary to make the effort to understand the account that faith gives of itself in its own terms—just as we have insisted that the Christian must not try to short-circuit with slogans the difficult, and at times painful, effort to face the challenge of Marxist analysis. There is no possible relationship unless each recognises the autonomy of the other. There is a Marxist way of understanding Christianity, as there is a Christian way to see Marxism. But in order for these mutual challenges to be really fruitful, neither should try to reduce the other to a simple 'misunderstanding'. If there is to be—and we don't know it at present—a convergence, it must be 'in the truth' and not simply in the cleverness of argument or in the twilight of ambiguity. This is the reason why I have attempted to keep exposition of Marxist theory and theological insight in relatively independent formulations, not meeting in direct doctrinal polemics but in their encounter in concrete historical situations.

The ultimacy of love

The Christian faith affirms the ultimacy and engaged character of love. A few comments are necessary to clarify this affirmation.

1. Love is ontologically ultimate. I think this is one of the ways in which we can express the meaning of the fundamental Christian understanding of God: the Trinity. Trinitarian doctrine is not an explicit Biblical formulation. It is a focus which the Church has found in order to read organically what the Scripture says about God's action and purpose. And it has proved, I think, a right and necessary focus. In relation to our theme, Trinitarian doctrine means at least three things:

In the first place, it means that there is no way of going 'behind' or 'beyond' the self-assertion that God has given of himself in his own action and Word. There is no undifferentiated 'ground of being', no universally discoverable 'reason', no unnamed 'energy' to which we can appeal or from which we can derive or to which we could trace the concrete will and purpose which has been manifested in the history of God's self-revelation. He is as he has acted — in creation, in Jesus Christ, in the power of his Spirit. The concrete threeness and unity of an active love is the ultimate reality.

Secondly, 'three' has to be taken in the strong sense in which it appears in the Bible and it has been affirmed particularly in the eastern tradition. It is important to say this because Western Christian theology since Augustine, haunted by an individualistic conception of personality and an obsession with an ultimate unitary rational principle, has tended to reduce the Trinity to 'a way of speaking', a metaphor, and to rob it of its explosive and revolutionary content. The unity of the Trinity is not a denial of real differentiation: this is why we must insist on 'three persons' and understand the expression 'one substance' in terms of the Johannine characterisation 'God is love'. Our God is not a solitary Power looking at itself, a monologuing philosopher in Heaven: it is the Father, Son and Holy Spirit in the deepest oneness that can exist, the oneness of immediate, unambiguous and total love. In God, to have one's own being in the relation to the other is not a diminution of being but the plenitude of reality.

Finally, it is in the light of this understanding that we have to look at God's power: the centre of power is shared love, the shared love of the Father, the Son and the Holy Spirit. The dynamic of reality is not the absolute self-enclosed *potentia* our conceptions, derived from an imperial understanding of power, have presupposed—and which can only end in blessing capitalist grasping and Machiavellian politics. The ultimate basis of power is absolute solidarity and mutual sharing. For this reason, the Christian proclamation of love is not a voluntaristic or moralistic appeal, as humanist idealism has it. Love does not rest in our will, or in a projected dream born of the imagination. We are not calling men to 'invent' or 'create' a reality which does not exist, but to be what they are, to come to themselves—personally and collectively—children of ultimate, shared and communicated love.

2. Love is historically concrete and engaged. In Biblical terms, the Triune God is the god of the covenant. Liberal rationalistic theology has always found the idea of the covenant a stumbling block because their god was an essence, a principle or an energy and these things are capable of being participated in, incorporated or contemplated, but cannot enter into living, committed, concrete historical relationships. Scriptures, on the other hand, know only such relationships: God calls man into being and addresses him in terms of promises, tasks and limitations. The whole Biblical narrative is a record of these 'covenants'—in Adam, Noah, Abraham, Moses and Jesus Christ.

We are not interested in a speculative theology of the covenants —Christian theology has suffered enough from it! The important thing here is what the 'covenantal relationship' tells us concerning the Triune God as the love that will not remain confined in itself but which is constantly moving outwards and creating new, concrete forms of engagement. The ultimacy of love—the Trinity

—and its engaged character—the covenant—are inseparable in Biblical terms. Karl Barth found an incisive formulation when he said that the Trinity is the implicit presupposition of the covenant and the covenant is the explicit expression of the Trinity. Three elements in the Biblical teaching about the covenantal relationship call for particular attention in terms of our subject. The first is that God does not want to be known— or rather, he will not let himself be known—outside this covenantal relationship: he discloses his 'name', he makes himself known by fulfilling his promises and judgments. This is the meaning of the well-known formula: 'When it . . . happens, *then you will know*.' The relationships that man fancies and fashions with his 'gods' are empty of reality and power; the true God fashions himself a relationship and can only be known within it. There is no neutral, objective, unengaged knowledge of God.[2]

Secondly, the covenant is always a communal relationship: it binds people together with God not as isolated individuals but as social entities. It is not merely a covenant *with* Adam, Noah or Moses; it is a covenant *in* Adam, Moses or Noah with the whole of humanity, or with a particular group of people for the sake of the whole. The relationship that God establishes involves, not merely as a consequence or as a deduction but in and of itself a human solidarity which becomes both promise and judgment. For this reason, finally, a covenant always includes certain specific obligations and requirements which involve human relationships: protection of life, fulfilment of the law, the practice of justice in concrete relationships are the extension to the partners in the covenant of the reality into which they are covenanted: the ultimate outgoing love—the Triune God. John is not therefore moralising but simply expounding this fundamental covenant relation when he says: 'He who does not love [his neighbour] does not know God, because God is love.'

3. Love encompasses and gives unity to the totality of man's relationship with God and with his neighbour. Although we cannot develop this idea, it is important to take a position concerning the relation of creation to redemption, because the failure to grasp both their unity and distinction has plagued Christian theology and had very grave consequences. Perhaps

the best way to put it succinctly is to point out that 'evil' is presented in Scripture in terms of this covenant relationship: it is not simply the expression of a bad will (Kant), or an absence or lack (Augustine in his neo-platonic formulations) but dis-honouring the relationships of the covenant in their concrete demands. In this respect, the story of the Fall must not be read in isolation but in the context of the dramatic presentation of Genesis 3–6 of the escalating dissolution of God's established relationships: man grasps for autonomy (Adam), disowns his brother (Cain), perverts the relationships of love (chapter 6) and unleashes violence and corruption. It is over against this inordi-nate and self-seeking 'grasping' of man which breaks the solidarity of the covenant that was invested in Adam, both as representing its origin and its totality, that we are to understand the meaning of 'the second Adam', Jesus Christ. He does not 'grasp' but offers himself, thus reverting the process of man's self-destruc-tion and inaugurating a new relationship, the new covenant in which utter self-giving solidarity (love) is the absolute law.

The unity of creation and redemption is found, therefore, in this covenant solidarity of love and responsibility. Redemption does not abrogate the relationships of creation, it does not detach man from God's world: it reinstates this relationship both in the sense of restoring to man the right to be man—forgiveness— —and of disclosing the ultimate meaning of man's place in creation: the active solidarity of love. Redemption gives man back to creation and creation to man. For this reason, Paul says, 'the whole creation groans . . . and is in travail . . . straining towards the manifestation of the sons of God' (Romans 8:19–22). To this unity and differentiation we shall return in a moment.

From this very fragmentary formulation of the Christian understanding of God we can begin to put in perspective two important questions that emerged in our discussion of Marx's atheism. The first is the disjunctive God/man in which he affirms man and is therefore led to reject God. Hence his admiration for Prometheus. But in Christian terms God himself is Prometheus —he himself undertakes on the side of man and in the utter solidarity of love the restoration of man's right and power to be free in the world: he himself fights for man's lordship and, 'although we do not yet see that all things have been subjected to him (man), we see him (Jesus Christ) crowned with honour and glory' (Hebrews 2:8b–9), the promise and assurance of man's final liberation and glory.[3]

This immediately raises the other problem decisive for Marx: mediation. Why do we need to project on a (historical or mythological) figure, Jesus Christ, what belongs to man himself? A serious consideration of this question — which we have to leave aside now — requires at least three approaches. The first is the discussion of the need for mediation as a human, concrete question. It seems to me that a Marxist–Leninist tenet such as, for instance, the necessary role of a 'party of the proletariat', is a clear indication that mediation belongs to the nature of any historical movement, at least in the present alienated condition of man and society. There need not be any fundamental discrepancy at this point. A second question places us at a different — and now definitely divergent — level: the nature of alienation. If alienation is a radical fact which appears in different historical forms — and undoubtedly Marxist analysis has laid bare some of them in an incisive way — but roots back in a fundamental estrangement, then mediation must also be radical. In other words, man cannot save himself. This leads to a final point in this respect: the nature of Christ's mediation. I think that the German woman theologian Dorothee Sölle has established a valuable distinction between a 'substitute' and a 'representative'. The former replaces and absorbs the person and initiative of those whom he substitutes, the latter takes up the temporarily necessary function of doing, on behalf of the represented — a minor, an incapacitated, a powerless person or group — that which he or they cannot do, *in order that they may arrive at the point at which they may themselves do it*. He intends to do this in such a way that the represented may be objectively and subjectively empowered. Man has not been cancelled or replaced by Christ: he has been reinstated in a covenant relationship in which he will 'grow into full maturity', i.e., grow into the fullness of creativity, freedom, fellowship which Jesus himself displayed and made available. The mediation of Christ is not the substitution of man (although substitutive once-for-all aspects are not excluded):

it is the restitution of man as God's free and active agent in God's humanising purpose. Given the radical view of man's alienation, this process of redemption becomes a history of struggle which will not cease until the end. When Christ's lordship becomes finally visible and totally operative, man will be really man, the solidary and creative creature that God created.

The power and efficacy of solidary love

This process is an eschatological one. But it determines the nature of Christian action—the nature of Christian ethics, which we can summarise as the search for ways of realising concretely in the world the power and efficacy of solidary love. Such an ethic can only be achieved if we succeed in releasing the Christian understanding of love from its idealistic, subjectivistic and sentimental distortions; in other words, to rescue it from its bourgeois captivity. In order to do this we need to recover the Biblical context of love.

1. Biblical love is defined in its intention by God's active purpose: the establishment of his Kingdom, the sovereignty of his covenantal, humanising love. When Jesus himself defined his own mission, he did it in terms of the prophetic tradition:

> The Spirit of the Lord is upon me, because he has anointed me to preach good news to the poor. He has sent me to proclaim release to the captives and recovering of sight to the blind, to set at liberty those who are oppressed, to proclaim the acceptable year of the Lord (Luke 4:18 ff.).

The background of this programme is the jubilee tradition and the prophetic promise of God's ultimate peace—his *shalom*—a very rich expression which embraces the total welfare of the individual and the community: health, abundance, just relations, prosperity, harmonious family relations, personal fulfilment, faithfulness to God, a just government. The promise of peace reaches in the prophetic message a totalising character including the total harmony of creation, so beautifully expressed in the Psalm:

Steadfast love and faithfulness will meet: righteousness and peace will kiss each other. Faithfulness will spring up from the ground, and righteousness will look down from the sky. Yea, the Lord will give what is good, and our land will yield its increase. Righteousness will go before him, and make his footsteps a way. (Psalm 85:10–12).

The ministry of our Lord is the enactment of this programme: healing and preaching, feeding the hungry and forgiving sins, defeating death and subduing nature are not mere manifestations of power, they are the fulfilment of the messianic promise, the signs of the powerful breaking in of the Kingdom.

The apostolic ministry carries on this movement. But here a new element is bound to appear: the apostolic ministry cannot be a direct continuation of Christ's because the apostles are not Christ—their witness has a new reference, the reconciling work of the Lord himself in whom this programme has become a reality among men. Therefore the apostle proclaims the Kingdom in Jesus Christ and calls us to faith in him. This is the salutary mediation which we have just indicated. A Christian ethics has as its ultimate horizon the *shalom* of the Kingdom and as its immediate criterion and power the redemptive mediation of Jesus Christ.

The indissoluble unity of this horizon and the mediation are the heart of Christian witness. Faith, therefore, has its object in Jesus Christ and its concreteness in God's Kingdom. Repentance, conversion and sanctification—man's conscious commitment to the covenant—are therefore always concrete. This is illustrated in the Gospels with sharp and at times painful clarity. When salvation enters the house of Zaccheus, he immediately rectifies his whole life: returns what he has grasped and reforms his conduct; the rich young ruler, on the other hand, cannot follow Christ because he loves his riches and cannot part with them. Believing in Christ—says the Book of Acts—opens the new Christian community to the brother: they sell what they have and use the money for the common needs. But it condemns Ananias and Zaphira because they want to reserve for themselves in isolation something which belongs to the total availability of faith. A Christian has to 'renounce the works of darkness' which are very specifically described by the Apostle as that which breaks the solidary community of love: hatred, avarice (which is idolatry!), quarrelling, self-seeking, the concupiscence of the eye and the grasping desire for the world. There is no abstract, immaterial faith because the object and the source of faith is the humanising power of God's love.[4]

2. It is further to be noted that, both in the prophetic tradition and in the proclamation and the ministry of the Lord, the work of peace is described as the healing and liberation of the oppressed and afflicted. In other words, love operates in this alienated world by establishing justice. And justice is not measured by some impartial or legal regulations but by the redressing of the condition of the weak. Kings are judged throughout the whole Old Testament by a two-fold criterion: whether they faithfully led their people in the worship of the Lord and whether they did justice to the poor. A King rules 'according to Yahweh's heart' if 'he judged rightly the cause of the poor, the widow, the orphan and the foreigner'—those who have no human protection. Because, since the violent death of Abel, the Lord has himself taken the cause of the oppressed as his own: he is the *go'el* (the avenger and the liberator) of all those who suffer arbitrarily. Justice is the cutting edge of love. And this inevitably involves love in conflict, a permanent feature of both the prophetic and the dominical ministries. Judgment, therefore, is the unavoidable shadow of love as it meets human arrogance and inhumanity. And the seriousness of this judgment is such that it becomes final, ultimate:

'Depart from me, you cursed, into the eternal fire prepared for the devil and his angels; for I was hungry and you gave me no food, I was thirsty and you gave me no drink, I was a stranger and you did not welcome me, sick and in prison and you did not visit me,' . . . 'Truly I say to you, as you did it not to one of the least of these, you did it not to me'. And they will go away into eternal punishment. (Matthew 25:41–42, 45).

The disciplines of effectiveness

There is no mistaking the direction of these teachings.

Probably most Christians would accept that this is so. There is hardly a possibility of constructing the Biblical teaching in a different sense — although our clever hermeneutics have frequently found ways of taming it! Christian ethics, nevertheless, faces still a crucial problem: how do we do justice effectively in the world? The hungry, thirsty, naked, foreigners and prisoners of the world are always historical beings, caught in the web of human economic, political, social relationships. Our obligation to them cannot escape the complexity of such relationships. In other words, Christian ethics has to deal with the problem of historical mediation. We cannot at this point simply reproduce Biblical models because we live in a different world. Just as we cannot pattern our temples or write our poetry and music after the model of Hebrew architecture, poetry or music, we cannot exercise charity in the manner of the eighth century B.C. or the first century A.D. The mediation of a contemporary sociology, politics, economy is just as indispensable as that of a modern architecture, literature or medicine, although much more difficult and perplexing. We must examine some aspects of the problem.

1. The need for some form of historical mediation is not new for Christian ethics. It has assumed several forms which we cannot now discuss in detail, although it is useful to remember them. There has been the attempt to apply Old Testament law directly, as in Calvin's Genevan regulations, or the New Testament indications as in some Anabaptist groups. The problem has been that, as these regulations relate to sociological conditions which do not obtain any longer or are illustrations and pointers rather than law, they cannot be directly transposed but require a certain modification and this is the way in which the interests of those concerned or the actual uses of society are unwittingly smuggled in as divine law. The scholastic idea of 'natural law', inspired by Greek Stoic philosophy, attempts a middle way, seeking for a coincidence between divine law (as given, for instance, in the Mosaic covenant) and laws discovered by reason. There is no doubt that significant ethical contributions have been made from this perspective — for instance laws regulating war, or penal law, or the introduction of certain humane criteria

in the master/servant relationship. But again the lack of awareness of historical conditioning left this ethic unprotected against the temptation of passing as divine or natural law what was only the expression of interests or the balance of power. The Lutheran doctrine of 'the two realms' was a definite effort to protect the autonomy of the secular realm. In Luther's own view such autonomy was not absolute: on the one hand, the secular realm was also under the sovereignty of God and, although it was the realm of law and power, it was directed to the protection of human life and the ordering of society in peace and justice; on the other hand, the Christian was 'called' to exercise his love through his participation in the secular society. But Luther's defences were too weak to withstand the pressures of the turbulent times of the building up of capitalism, and the doctrine of the two realms was easily distorted to the profit of the new bourgeoisie in two complementary ways: on the one hand, the secular kingdom was excluded from all religious control or criticism, a battlefield for a no-hold-barred power struggle; on the other hand, the exercise of Christian love was reduced to the interpersonal forms of charity, cancelling out a fundamental dimension of the Biblical witness. The tragic results were the vulnerability of a large sector of the German churches to the Nazi tyranny. Or the way in which capitalism was able to clear its way from all religious interferences and give to the enterprising Christian of the eighteenth and nineteenth centuries the possibility of transporting slaves in the hold of his ship while composing hymns on the deck, or exploiting children's labour and punctiliously giving his tithe to the Church or founding orphanages for workers' children while opposing the formation of trade unions as an invention of the devil.

2. A self-righteous indignation will not serve as an adequate response to these painful facts of our history. It may indeed be the best way to avoid coming to terms with the problem. The crux of the matter is that Christian ethics has lacked — quite understandably until recent times and quite ideologically at present — an instrument for analysing the real dynamics of society and assessing the churches' active role in it. Therefore, the articulation of Christian love has been haphazard, arbitrary and

sentimental and has easily fallen prey to the interests, 'very secular' as Marx said, of those in power. It is in this respect, I think, where a Christian ethics can — and indeed I would say must — take Marxism seriously. It offers a scientific, verifiable and efficacious way to articulate love historically.

I have argued that the search for a historically scientific way of making love efficacious is the ethos of Marxism. If this is true, the use of the Marxist analysis is not something foreign for the Christian. Our real discrepancy has to do with the ultimate nature and foundation of that love. And this is not without practical consequences. But the intention to make this love historically operative for the total human society is essential for both Christian and Marxist. This is the foundation of the 'strategic alliance' which Fidel Castro called for. In such alliance the Marxist is forced to lay bare and open for discussion the source and power of his love. But the Christian is forced to acknowledge his lack of a scientific historical mediation and to receive it, critically but not ungratefully. On the other hand, as Visser 't Hooft suggested twenty-five years ago, here lies also the impossibility of a Christian's 'strategic alliance' with capitalism. For, quite apart from whatever humane aspects it may have picked up in its later developments, the basic ethos of capitalism is definitely anti-Christian: it is the maximising of economic gain, the raising of man's grasping impulse, the idolising of the strong, the subordination of man to the economic production. Humanisation is for capitalism an unintended by-product, while it is for socialism an explicit goal. Solidarity is for capitalism accidental; for socialism, it is essential. In terms of their basic ethos, Christianity must criticise capitalism radically, in its fundamental intention, while it must criticise socialism functionally, in its failure to fulfil its purpose.

This does not mean, of course, a blind acceptance of Marxist analysis and ideology. Features like class-struggle, the dictatorship of the proletariat or the role of the Communist Party are in part a piece of analytic theory which, with all due correction and revision, have to play a part in a Christian's articulation of his love-seeking-for-justice. But they are also ideological slogans which bear the mark of a conception of man and history which the Christian cannot fully accept. The Christian alliance with Marxist socialism is therefore always an uneasy alliance, in which the fundamental divergence about the source and power of solidary love results in constant questioning in the realm of practice. But it is important now to emphasise that the source of this criticism is not a rejection of Marxism as social theory but a radical questioning of the philosophical foundation of its ethos —the rejection of the Triune God of love.

In this respect there must be no confusion. Let me illustrate it in closing by drawing from one of the more humanist articulations of Marxist solidary love, the work of the psychologist and philosopher Erich Fromm.[5] From a psychological point of view, Fromm distinguishes 'unproductive' and 'productive' characters. It is in the second type where man fulfils his humanity, where he reaches 'the goal of human development'. When he attempts to define more precisely the idea of 'productivity', he uses the expression 'productive love'. This is the authentic form of human existence. Furthermore, he finds in love the answer to the tension, always present in human experience, between fellowship and 'separationism' (to be myself over against others). Here, while capitalism makes fellowship dependent on individualism, socialism finds personhood dependent on solidarity.[6] Other features of an authentic love, according to Fromm, are no less acceptable from a Christian point of view: the distinction between love and sentimentalism, the view of love as an active exercise of man's will, the need to relate the exercise of love to the structures and dynamic of society, the emphasis on concentration, discipline and patience, the analysis of love in terms of care, responsibility, respect and knowledge, the warning against standard recipes, the unmasking of the perversions of human life when it moves around a different centre—namely irresponsible self-concern instead of productive love.

But then, the difference emerges. Fromm himself points it out: for him, man's love for himself, his self-affirmation (to be distinguished, to be sure, from egoism, which is the immoderate and exclusive concentration on oneself) is the basis of productive love. Man constitutes himself by determining, without any external authority, although certainly in the context of society, the goals and meaning of his existence. Hence, he rejects all 'love of God' which would not be, in the last resort, man's return to himself as a human being—'all gods who will not recognise man's self-consciousness as the highest divinity', as Marx had said. This is, according to Fromm, the only possible humanistic ethic. Anything else is alienation, because 'man owes to himself his existence, not only materially but also emotionally and intellectually'. It is quite evident that we move here on a ground radically different from the Christian faith. For the latter, man is constituted as man in a relationship to God and the neighbour which is not 'added' to his autonomy but belongs to his very existence as human. Love is not a product of man but man a product of love. A Christian can, therefore, ask whether the Marxist search for a concrete and effective expression in history of solidary love does not lead to something much deeper and total. And, therefore, whether man's alienation does not require a deeper and more radical remedy. For Christians, the ultimate answer is God's own love who has 'productively' assumed human existence in order to open it up, through his own self-giving, to a new form of existence. This does not eliminate but, on the contrary, calls for specific forms of historical mediation. It places them in the perspective of a larger and permanent movement, until we reach the new heavens and the new earth, the city with foundations, of which God is the builder and maker.

CHAPTER VIII

THE PROMISE AND THE LIMITS OF THE ALLIANCE

THE ARGUMENT OF this book starts from the concrete fact of the common commitment of a significant number of Christians and Marxists in Latin America to a struggle for liberation which finds expression in a socialist project which, in different forms and measures, incorporates elements of Marxist analysis and ideology. I have pointed out that this 'strategic alliance' is one of the major facts in the Latin American situation—a rather startling and baffling one for many and at times a very tense and challenging one for those involved. It has been my attempt throughout our discussions to analyse the conditions of this relationship. I have tried not to lose sight of the fact that I was dealing with a reality, not outlining a theoretical possibility. But, at the same time, unless one takes a purely pragmatic attitude, such a fact cannot be accepted uncritically: it must be explored in its motivations, its implications, its possibilities and weaknesses. And this requires the careful study of both the theoretical assumptions and the practical courses of action which the words 'Christian' and 'Marxist' connote and denote.

The result of our attempt at such a study can be summarised in four basic points:

(1) For both Christians and Marxists, knowledge is not a theoretical contemplation of abstract truths but a concrete engagement, an active relationship with reality. For the Marxist, this is a specific revolutionary action; for the Christian, historical

praxis takes place in the context and under the demands of a covenant relationship which God himself has opened and defined for us. But in both cases neutral, purely objective, precommitted or uncommitted knowledge is an impossibility.

(2) Christians and Marxists share (according to my interpretation, at least) an ethos of human solidarity. They see mankind as directed towards a form of life in which every member of society fully participates in all the possibilities afforded by nature and human relationships. There is a basic difference in the way in which Christians and Marxists conceive the dynamics and the outcome of history. But the common ethos of human solidarity unites them in their opposition to an inhuman and oppressive organisation of society and human life, and in the search for justice as the immediate concrete demand of love. Because of this deep difference we cannot speak of 'unity'. But because of the common concern we can speak not of mere 'tactical' co-operation—in which each one uses the other for his own purposes—but of a 'strategic alliance' in which there is a common immediate—though limited—goal.

(3) Christians can agree with Marxists on the need for a historical mediation of our humanist intention, i.e. for a set of analytic tools, a concrete political and social programme and a coherent ideological view which permits men to embrace and carry forward the struggle for human liberation. Although there are many points at which the Marxist analysis, programme and ideology can and must be corrected, revised or perfected (and in such an effort all men can co-operate), a Christian can accept such elements as substantially accurate and valuable.

(4) The ultimate horizons of the Christian and Marxist ethos are radically different—they see the source and the power of solidary love in mutually exclusive ways. Such a difference projects itself on our 'strategic alliance' making it a tense and mutually challenging one. For the Christian this is neither accidental nor a particular feature of his relation to Marxism, but a tension built into all his life in history until the Parousia of the Lord. It does not lead him to renounce the historical exercise of solidary love, but to bring constantly to bear on it the perspective of faith.

Having these conclusions in mind we must now return to the examination of the relationship and see how it can be critically clarified, corrected and made more significant. This formulation corresponds, to be sure, to a certain option which I share with many Christians in my continent and which I tried to formulate in the preface, by saying that I was convinced that 'a revolutionary action aiming at changing the basic economic, political, social and cultural structures and conditions of life is imperative today in the world', and that I considered that 'the forms of economic analysis, the insight into the dynamics of history and the revolutionary ethos of Marxism are—however corrected or reinterpreted—indispensable for such a revolutionary change'. In the light of our discussion and this option I shall now briefly explore three areas: (1) the terms of the relations between Christians and Marxists; (2) the specific nature of Christian participation in revolution; (3) a Christian 'spirituality' that corresponds to this relationship. We shall deal with the first two issues in this chapter and leave the third for the last chapter. We shall offer only very sketchy and tentative suggestions, because actually these things can only be considered in concrete situations and worked out historically.

Can a Christian be a Marxist?

Is it possible to speak of 'a Christian Marxist' or 'a Marxist Christian'? A very committed left-wing journal in Chile entitled an editorial two years ago: 'Neither Christian socialists nor socialist Christians'. The point was: we are not a particular brand of socialists—namely Christians; 'Christian' is not an adjective. But neither are we a special brand of Christians—namely socialist; 'socialist' is not an adjective either. Both words represent autonomous commitments at different levels of experience. We are Christians *and* socialists. Father Lawrence Bright makes the same point:

A Christian has to recognise, first of all, that in itself Christianity is not enough; it can only be realised in a practical way through detailed analysis and strategy. But the detailed analysis and strategy which Marxism provides must then

be judged, however critically, in its own terms; the Christian
who accepts some form of Marxism judges it as a Marxist,
not specifically as a Christian [although he does not have to
modify his Christian faith in order to do it: his objectives as
Christian are compatible with the analysis]; he does not have
to be a special sort of Christian, a Marxist Christian. But
neither does he have to be a special sort of Marxist, a Christian
Marxist. This is the point at which many Christians get
stuck. They are prepared, today, to end the cold war with the
Marxist groups and to enter into dialogue, but they are not
prepared to take the necessary step beyond ecumenism and
join the other side. Partly, this is a historical problem of the
West. To be a Christian and a Marxist is normal enough in, for
example, South America where the culture is Catholic but the
social situation is sufficiently bad to make revolution an
obvious necessity. When one is dispossessed one is not a
revolutionary simply on principle; what has to be done is clear,
and one sets about doing it without waiting for justification
from the Christian gospel or Marxist philosophy. One is
Christian and Marxist because that's how things are.[1]

The point made here is an important and valid one. It intends
to preserve both the integrity and the autonomy of faith and
political engagement. But it is not unambiguous because both
Marxism and Christianity make total claims which overflow
this clear distinction of levels. It seems to me, therefore, that a
greater clarity is needed, not in order to obstruct real co-operation,
but precisely to make it genuinely possible.

Can a Christian be a Marxist? We must face the multiplicity of
meanings of the word 'Marxist' or, to put in other, less assuming
terms, the different possibilities of articulating this question.
It is possible, in the first place, to consider Marxism exclusively
as a set of analytic tools concerning economic activity and its
political and social significance. Such tools make it possible to
analyse capitalist society and bourgeois culture in a dynamic way
and therefore to project a political strategy of change. It is even
possible in this respect to receive the Marxist criticism of
religion — as we did it partially in previous chapters — as a valid

instrument for understanding and criticising bourgeois Christianity and therefore as a valuable contribution to a true renewal of the churches. This rather instrumental understanding of Marxism has not only been accepted by some Christians but also by many revolutionaries and political leaders in the Third World, who would not declare themselves Marxists but would freely recognise that their programme and policies are deeply indebted to Marxist theory and analysis. In this respect, one may go further and say that Marxist insights, like any other scientific discovery, are now a generally available resource and, as such, it is not only legitimate for the Christian to use it, but he is morally obligated so to do to the extent that it proves to be scientifically accurate and valuable.

But few Marxists would be satisfied with such a description of their position. They would rightly claim that Marxism is not a neutral scientific tool but a revolutionary theory and a revolutionary movement, and that this is part and parcel of the scientific analysis itself. It is true that there are various interpretations of Marxist revolutionary theory and conflicting movements claiming the right to represent a 'correct' Marxist position. But I think we must admit that there is a basic conception of the socialist revolution, the role of the working class and the nature of the revolutionary process that can recognisably be called Marxist and that has played a decisive role in all revolutionary movements since the latter part of the last century. I am including in this characterisation such widely different revolutionary conceptions as that of Cuba, Yugoslavia, China and the Tanzanian form of socialism, to give names that define a very ample range. In so far as a Christian commits himself to participate in a socialist historical project, he can scarcely avoid relating to Marxism within this wide spectrum. In concrete, he will quite likely join — certainly with different degrees of attachment — some movement, party or group in which Marxism will play a prominent if not leading role.

Certainly this poses some problems for a Christian, in so far as the programme of such movements reflects an understanding of reality which he does not fully share and — what seems to me more important — in so far as Marxist socialist revolutions so far have shown certain disquieting features in relation to personal freedom, popular participation, the control of power or the ability to overcome discrimination after the revolution. In joining a movement such as this, the Christian cannot but feel that he is helping to bring about conditions which are not entirely satisfactory. There is nothing new in such a plight: it is the common problem involved in all ethical action (or inaction for that matter) and it has always been recognised as attaching to the ethical dilemma of human life this side of the Parousia. Theological ethics has usually operated on the idea of 'the lesser evil'. I think it is far more significant to think in terms of 'the greater good' as well. In other words, history—and ethical action is conscious participation in history—must be seen by the Christian both in its discontinuity with God's Kingdom (and therefore as the sphere where evil can only be partially checked) and in its continuity (and therefore as the sphere in which the good of the Kingdom can be partially anticipated). A significant and growing number of Christians are becoming convinced—not only emotionally, nor arbitrarily, but on the basis of sober analysis— that on both accounts participation in a revolutionary socialist project is an ethically defensible and necessary action.

The fact should not be denied or underrated that many Christians are reluctant to take such action because of the radical criticism of the Christian religion and the belligerent attitude towards it that many Marxist movements and the most significant Marxist countries have taken. Concerning the criticism of religion, I think that, in so far as it is a criticism of alienating and perverted forms of Christianity, it should be received as an invitation for self-criticism, repentance and rebirth. The 'persecution' of religion in communist countries poses a number of other problems concerning the historical role of the Church, the nature of Constantinian Christianity, the class-captivity of some churches and many other questions which we cannot examine at this point. But the importance of this fact should not be minimised, nor the fact that Christians who join Marxist revolutionary movements or parties are frequently treated as 'second class' revolutionaries! While the self-righteous criticism of outsiders who are frequently—wittingly or unwittingly—supporting the capitalist *status quo* and acting as propaganda agents for it, cannot be taken too seriously, the Christians committed to revolution must openly reject these fascist trends in socialism, not only for the sake of the freedom of the Church to proclaim the gospel and of its members to act in society, but for the health of the revolutionary movement itself. On the other hand, our Latin American experience tends to show that, in so far as the reactionary associations of the churches are overcome, Marxism loses much of its anti-religious virulence.

It is frequently said today that the problem of violence is what deters—and should prevent—Christians from joining revolutionary movements. The question of violence is an urgent and serious one.[2] But the argument that we have just mentioned is clearly a fallacy, except for those Christians (who have always been a small but significant minority) who have interpreted the Christian faith in terms of absolute pacifism. Marxist belief that the socialist revolution will involve violence does not arise from an apotheosis of violence (which finds its historical place rather in fascist movements and theorists) but from the observation of the history of revolutionary movements. This is what is meant by the oft-quoted and misinterpreted sentence of Marx that 'violence is the midwife of history'. The Christian will certainly be concerned that the use of violence be kept to the minimum in any case. In such an effort he will be joined by many non-Christian revolutionaries. But it should give us pause that Christian ethicists who have seldom questioned the use of violence for the preservation of the existing order have not paid attention to the fact that the word 'violence' is almost exclusively applied in the Scriptures to the actions of unjust authorities (kings, priests, rich) and the oppressors of the people!

But we have to turn to a more difficult question: can a Christian be a Marxist in the sense of embracing historical and dialectical materialism? I have tried to argue that the answer to this question depends on the way in which these philosophical positions are understood. If materialism is interpreted as a criticism of idealism, it seems that it is not in itself inimical to the Christian faith. In many ways it is a salutary correction to the age-long and distorting alliance of Christian theology to philosophical idealism, which has given rise to a number of crippling theological and ethical interpretations of the Christian faith. Serious attention to historical materialism can have a very invigorating effect for Christian theology, although the Christian faith will not certainly accept the submission of its affirmations to conditions laid down by any philosophy. Unfortunately, one must immediately add that most Marxists – at least the most conspicuous – have claimed for materialism a totality and exclusiveness which negates in principle all reality which is not reduced to immanent terms. Such a claim Christians must reject, not because they speculatively pose the existence of a realm of the 'spirit' but because they have been grasped by the reality of the living God who is beyond history and the universe as well as active in history and the universe, the living God who in faith they know to be true, nay, to be *the* true and ultimate reality in which everything has meaning and existence. At this point, no compromise is possible. Actually, such a compromise would void the engagement of the Christian as such of all authenticity and meaning. A Christian cannot be a Marxist in this sense, unless the claims of Marxist philosophy are considered as relative rather than absolute (which, by the way, might well be a serious scientific attitude).

Can a Marxist be a Christian?

It is not for us to answer the question. I am tempted to limit myself to the answer that a Cuban Christian friend gave to a prominent communist leader who asked him whether he would be able to join the Communist Party: 'This', he said, 'is your problem, not mine.' As soon as a confessing Christian is admitted to the Communist Party, the definition of the party undergoes an interpretation. It is for the party to decide whether it wants to accept such an interpretation or not. When a Marxist becomes Christian he does not need to cease being a Marxist – this is the much misunderstood question of 'conversions', as if Marxism were a religion or Christianity an ideology. But he places his Marxism in a different context, against a different horizon, and therefore, to that extent, it inevitably modifies it.[3]

In fact, the answer can be given in a more direct – and perhaps, to some, more offensive — way: nobody (whether Marxist or not) can become a Christian without repentance and conversion. Not a conversion from Marx to the Church, but from sin to Jesus Christ. This movement entails a submission of the totality of life, including one's philosophical understanding or political allegiance, to the grace and the judgment of the Lord. If the argument of this book is valid, what is deepest and most relevant in Marxism — the commitment to solidary love, the analysis of reality, the availability for the cause of the oppressed — will be confirmed, strengthened and deepened. But nothing can be exempted from the purifying fire of submission and consecration to the Lord.

A specifically Christian contribution?

If Christians participate in a revolutionary process preponderantly directed in Marxist terms, is there any specific Christian contribution? Or is the Christian faith only a motivating force? This question — which is raised sometimes by participants and most frequently by observers — cannot be solved, I think, in a dogmatic way. Somebody has rightly said that Christians cannot charge in advance the fee for their co-operation; their contribution will become visible and articulated in their participation. But this does not mean that the question as to how is the Christian faith relevant in a revolutionary movement is a superfluous one. Our previous discussion has noted at least two aspects of this relevance. On the one hand, Christians are called to the exercise of solidary love — a faith that 'works itself out in love' motivates for participation, and love looks for a relevant historical mediation. On the other hand, to the extent that the Christian religion has been co-opted into the present oppressive structures and is constantly manipulated for their preservation, a Christian faith which has rediscovered its revolutionary vocation can explode this reactionary instrumentalising of Christianity from within and thus unblock the conscience of Christians for an effective revolutionary participation.

There is, I think, a third point of articulation which deserves to be mentioned — although space does not permit to pursue it in any systematic way: it is the inspiring and critical power of the Christian faith. The Peruvian theologian Gustavo Gutiérrez has provided a most valuable framework of analysis by identifying two different levels in the process of liberation.[4] There is the level of political action, which is rational and scientific. But there is also the level of utopia, in which man projects his quest for a new man and a new society. The relation between these two elements is very delicate and important: utopia without political science is romantic, ineffective day-dreaming; science without a mobilising dream is inhuman or merely functional. The relation is even deeper. Science, by analysing and projecting the conditions and possibilities of the organisation of production, of political participation, of technological progress constantly opens up new fields for human fulfilment. Utopian thinking, projecting these possibilities in terms of its own vision of a new man and a new society, stimulates science to further adventure and discovery and puts forward a project which requires new hypotheses and new instruments. This process, which is not foreign even to physical sciences, is all the more important in social sciences.[5]

Faith, Gutiérrez continues, which is neither science nor utopian thinking but a living relationship with God and man, stirs utopian imagination by pushing in the direction of total fellowship. It holds before men the vision of the total, full manhood in perfect solidarity, freedom and availability, as it has been given to us in Christ. It presses towards the kingdom of peace and justice which has been promised and, in so doing, it invites utopian imagination to create, availing itself of the materials which human experience—and particularly the very experience of the struggle—throws up, new utopian projections which the revolution will make its own. Political, social and economic sciences, in turn, will try to analyse and project in concrete and effective ways such projections. In this way, faith becomes politically relevant through the stimulation of utopian thinking.

Gutiérrez's argument seems to me to be basically sound. History bears out his claim concerning the stimulating power of faith to spur man on to utopian thinking whenever the objective conditions make new possibilities for human life imaginable. The very birth of socialist utopianism is not foreign to this process. I think it is also correct to say that Christianity does not have in itself a political theory and much less a scientific set of tools for social analysis and economic planning. Faith is a relationship, an active engagement in a covenant. But it is also important to point out that it is not an *empty* relationship; it has a definite content, which is given by him in whom the relationship finds its basis and power, the Triune God of love. In this sense, the stimulus of faith is not an undefined dynamism which can be filled by no matter what vision of man and society. It has a direction which, as we have seen, is defined by God's purpose: his Kingdom of peace and justice. Therefore, it seems that faith stimulates utopian imagination in a positive and critical sense in at least three different ways:

1. As the Marxist Ernst Bloch has said, Biblical faith is the matrix of hope. The future is for faith never a closed horizon but always an effective promise. In the beautiful words of Jürgen Moltmann:

> From first to last, and not merely in the epilogue, Christianity is eschatology, is hope, forward looking and forward moving, and therefore also revolutionising and transforming the present. The eschatology is not one element *of* Christianity, but it is the medium of Christian faith as such, the key in which everything in it is set, the glow that suffuses everything here in the dawn of an expected new day . . . That is why faith, wherever it develops into hope, causes not rest but unrest, not patience but impatience . . . Peace with God means conflict with the world, for the goad of the promised future stabs inexorably into the flesh of every unfulfilled present . . . It makes the Church the source of continual new impulses towards the realisation of righteousness, freedom and humanity here in the light of the promised future that is to come.[6]

The bold humanistic affirmation that man's creative possibilities are unlimited, that it is possible to envisage and to accomplish far beyond the present, seemingly fixed, frontiers, that nature and the world and society can be stamped with the human imprint has a firm foundation only in God's promise and power. Christ is

risen indeed. Death, sin and the devil have been defeated. Their hold has been decisively broken. We can move forward in hope.
2. But a second and critical point must also be raised. Against every evolutionary idealism, faith looks at history as the arena of a permanent — although not undecisive — conflict. Christian eschatology prompts us to move in the direction of the Kingdom, but it also leads us to recognise the penultimate and partial character of all our achievements. The coming of the Kingdom will gather up and fulfil all legitimate human hope and all authentic action of love, but it will not be the mere addition of human hopes and efforts but God's own sovereign and final act of redemption, the coming of 'that same Jesus' in judgment and fulfilment. This recognition of the conflictive character of history — not merely temporarily and as a result of an inadequate organisation of society or an obsolete form of ownership — has important consequences in relation to the revolutionary process, which I think it is important to point out.

Basically, it means that there can be no 'teleological suspension of ethics'; in other words, no human class, group or generation can be considered as merely instrumental. This does not mean that revolutionary change may not involve inflicting suffering or that a certain sober 'calculation' and acceptance of human 'cost' can be excluded. It means, precisely, that such calculations of human cost and suffering cannot be separated from human, ethical considerations. It cannot be merely a question of tactics. And this for two reasons: One is that no human group or class can be made the exclusive and definitive bearer of evil in history. Evil is a solidary and total responsibility of mankind, and if it is true that it finds historical embodiment within specific conditions and that a class or a nation can be the typical and dominant representative of it at a certain point in history, it is also true that it cannot erase the power of the risen Christ present in all humanity, nor excuse our own responsibility for all of mankind. Wherever there is a human face there is evil and hope, and therefore ethical considerations must be upheld. Secondly, because a revolutionary process is not for the Christian the 'final sprint' in which humanity can exhaust the last human and moral breath, but only a stage — however important — in a long and continuously conflictive pilgrimage. Every generation, therefore, is at the same time means and end, the bearer of sacrifice and the inheritor of hope, called to realise as fully as possible all the human possibilities open to it (politically, socially, economically, spiritually) and called to suffer and to toil for new and greater possibilities for future generations. No really human achievement can be obtained through the denial of the humanity of some men or of a generation.

3. The point that we have been trying to establish seems significant for the discussion of some important aspects of Marxist revolutionary theory. The question is not that Christians have a monopoly of ethical insight while Marxists are unaware of them. If some expressions like that of Lenin's ('good is what advances the cause of the revolution') can give, outside its context, the impression of ethical superficiality, it will be easy to prove that Lenin himself, not to speak of Marx, were by no means insensitive to moral considerations. On the other hand, Marxists like Rosa Luxemburg, have devoted most reflection to the ethical questions which arise in the revolutionary struggle. The task of Christians concerned with revolutionary change is to participate actively in this reflection bringing to bear on it the peculiar insight which is born of faith, but willing to acknowledge and to own what other revolutionaries have developed. I want to mention four areas where these questions are particularly important.

There is the problem of means and ends. M.Rubel[7] has shown that Marx was deeply interested—and this precisely in the more mature and scientific work—in this question both in a theoretical and a practical way. He rightly rejects an idealistic perspective which poses ideal ends without incorporating in this reflection the actual dynamic of concrete reality. But he insists that human action is characterised by the ability to plan purposeful action, to incorporate rational goals into everyday activity. For this reason, he rejects all opportunistic action (such as that suggested at times by Lasalle) in which the revolutionary intention does not impregnate strategy and tactics at every point. But, as Rubel himself has pointed out, neither Marx nor Lenin carried far or deeply enough the consideration of the quality of action which corresponds to the nature of the society which they discern for the future. A realistic consideration of the relation between means and ends, such as Rosa Luxemburg intended in discussion with Lenin, is a still incomplete and urgent task. What are the consequences for revolutionary action of this pregnant sentence of Marx: 'If man is shaped by circumstances, it follows that it is necessary to give to them [circumstances] a human form'?[8]

It seems to me that a discussion of the relation between solidarity and hatred in revolutionary action is one of the problems which cannot be evaded. Christians must avoid moralising and self-righteousness when they discuss this issue. Enmity and hatred are not absent from the pages of the Bible; they are unashamedly attributed to the pioneers of the faith, and even to God himself. The dialectics of love and rejection is in the Bible much more complex than what is suggested by the usual admonition to 'hate evil but to love the evil-doer'. But how can rejection and active opposition, indeed hatred of the enemy which at a certain point incarnates the forces of injustice and inhumanity, be made in reality an instrument of love and redemption? How can they be neutralised in their long-term de-humanising effects on the revolutionary forces and on the end result of revolution? How can the humanity of the enemy be preserved in the process of combating him?

One way to pose this problem is the discussion of the meaning and nature of the dictatorship of the proletariat and the suppression of the oppressing class. Class war does not occur without subjective animosity and 'individually' unmerited suffering. The objective inequality which a revolutionary process creates should not, nevertheless, be glamourised as moral vindication, least of all clothed with the eschatological colours of a final judgment. For all their indignation at the exploitation of the proletariat and their hatred for the oppressors, Marx and Engels were quite conscious of this need. They realised that the objective 'privileges' of a dominant class—the proletariat in the socialist revolution—were a necessary stage determined by the nature of social dynamics. In this sense, Engels goes as far as saying that, to a certain extent, the class privileges of the bourgeoisie had 'a certain historical justification', not as a moral fact, but in the objective necessities of a process of expansion of production, which are a condition for arriving at a superior stage in the history of mankind.[9] Extrapolating this concept, one should add that the stage of 'the dictatorship of the proletariat' (and the unavoidable manipulation of human needs and suppression of human aspirations that it entails) should be regarded as transitory. Hence, revolutionaries should aim at building within the structures of the new society, the mechanisms that will hasten the overcoming of that stage and the alleviation of the burdens that it imposes. One may doubt that these considerations have been given enough weight in the revolutionary movements which have already taken place. Without sentimentalism or naivete, all genuine revolutionaries should be concerned with this problem.

This brings us to the last point, the problem of the control of power. The point is not the denial of class-struggle, nor of the fact that in a revolution the oppressed class must take firm control of power and vigorously counteract internal and external forces that fight for the reversal of the process. Sentimentalism and shallow humanitarianism—an empty pseudo-democratic affirmation of 'fair play' and 'equality'—can only be instruments of reaction and the cause of even greater suffering. But it must also be said that Marxist political thinking has not yet developed adequate forms of control of the exercise of power in order to prevent arbitrariness, the 'cult of personality', the appropriation by a clique or a bureaucracy of a total control of society, the exclusion of the very proletariat from the shaping of the process and the determination of its direction. Whether this inability should be attributed to the difficult circumstances that usually surround a revolution or to a naive confidence in the 'innocence' of the revolutionary class, or to an inadequate understanding of the responsibility of the 'party'—seen as an *avant-garde*—to the total proletariat, it is not for us to debate now. But as partakers in a revolutionary process we must—not only and not exclusively as Christians but as part and for the sake of the revolution itself—raise this problem and struggle for a more adequate solution.

CHAPTER IX

RED HEROES AND
CHRISTIAN MARTYRS

WITH SOME OF our considerations in the last chapter we have
already moved into a dimension which is not easily subject to
analytic thought: the level of attitudes, stances, approaches to
life which I will call, risking a broad and ambiguous word,
'spirituality'. Spirituality, in this sense, is a total way of life which
grows out of and surrounds any deep commitment. It is the
projection of a total engagement on everything that a man thinks,
does, dreams. As such, it is not an exclusively Christian phenomenon. We find it wherever we meet deep commitment, because
deep commitments are total: they affect all aspects of life and
subordinate everything to them. They make a total claim. Such
is, of course, the stuff of both heroism and fanaticism. J. B. S.
Haldane said that fanaticism is one of the only four important
inventions made between 3000 B.C. and A.D. 1400. And Eric
Hoffer comments: 'It was a Judaic-Christian invention. And it is
strange to think that in receiving this malady of the soul the
world also received a miraculous instrument for raising societies
and nations from the dead—an instrument of resurrection.'[1]

Whether total commitment to a cause is a malady or the only
possibility of human health can, of course, be debated. Christianity
and Marxism share the view that the latter is the case, however
they may differ in their understanding of the nature and demands
of this commitment. No honest observer will, in effect, deny that
Communism has developed a total commitment and a deep

'spirituality' in the sense we are using this word. Like all deep spiritualities, it becomes particularly visible and moving in relation to the frontiers of human life, the critical points: love, solitude, suffering, death. We cannot leave our consideration of the relation of Christians and Marxists within a revolutionary process without touching—however briefly—on the question of spirituality.

Communist heroes

What we have called spirituality can be roughly translated in Marxist terms by the notion of 'militancy'. To begin on the negative side, I may comment on the deep impression made on me by reading the biography of Josef Stalin by the—deeply opposed—Trotskyist Isaac Deutscher. Here is a person who can scarcely evoke spontaneous sympathy. He acts sometimes out of obscure and even inhuman motivations. Callousness, hatred, cynicism appear quite frequently in his words and actions. He will grasp for power and use it unashamedly. He will destroy, bend, overpower. He can be ruthless and cold. But one feels always in the presence of a man who, in his innermost being, has given himself to a cause, which is not always very clear and well defined (and therefore quite frequently turned into his own whim), but which masters his whole life. There is no frivolity, no equivocation, no possible relativising of this commitment. Whatever else he may be, he is—subjectively—a 'militant'.

I have chosen a rather perverse example, because it seems to me to indicate that communism, even at its worst, displays a depth which we cannot ignore. There is a seriousness which reminds us of the Puritan concentration on 'the one thing that matters', the exclusion of all that is superfluous or distracting in terms of the one purpose and goal. There is a total subordination of subjectivity and subjective feeling: love, family, artistic or emotional satisfaction, even one's own life and security—everything is 'counted as loss' for the sake of the cause. Sometimes we shudder at the ruthlessness of this total concentration. It is for us difficult to understand how a proud and intelligent Soviet theorist—like the ones who died under Stalin—will 'confess his mistakes' — obviously unreal — before the party, not in order to escape punishment, but because he knows that, in the long run, and in spite of himself, the party is right because the future belongs to it. Party discipline is not, for the militant, an external imposition: it is the core of his spirituality. However repulsive the manifestations of this total devotion may be, we have to respect them and to recognise that they have also appeared — both in their sublime and in their repugnant forms — at the crucial and most decisive points in the history of Christian spirituality. There is a hairbreadth line between fanaticism and devotion. Communism and Christianity have often illustrated both to a unique degree.

We could, of course, find innumerable examples of heroic and selfless devotion among Marxists. One thinks of the Italian hero Antonio Gramsci, living his death in Mussolini's prison and concentrating his last ounces of strength and lucidity to the cause of the proletariat of his country, without bitterness, totally consecrated to a future which he would not see. Or one can think of Ernesto (Ché) Guevara, forsaking his well-earned place of privilege and power in the triumphant Cuban revolution to risk his life every day in the Bolivian jungle. Ernst Bloch has celebrated the communist willingness to lay down their life in his epic of the 'red hero', the men who were killed for their opposition to Hitler in the concentration camps of Nazi Germany. His words are worth quoting because they reflect the depth and character of this total surrender:

All those who are sacrificed take to the tomb the flowers of yesterday, some of which are withered and unrecognisable. Only one category of man advances towards death almost totally dispossessed of all traditional consolation: he is the red hero. He confesses up to his death the cause for which he has lived and clearly, coldly, consciously, he advances towards that Nothingness in which he has learned to believe as a free spirit. His sacrifice is different from that of the ancient martyrs: these died almost without an exception with a prayer on their lips, confident that they had thus merited Heaven . . . But the Communist hero, whether under the Tsars, under Hitler or under any other power, sacrifices himself without hope of resurrection. His Good Friday is not sweetened—much less absorbed—by any Easter Sunday, a Sunday in which he will personally return to life. The Heaven to which the martyrs raised their arms amidst flames and smoke, does not exist for the red materialist. And nevertheless he dies confessing a cause, and his superiority can only be compared with that of the very early Christians or of John the Baptist.[2]

Nobody who is acquainted with the tortures, the suffering, the death of thousands of communist revolutionaries—as we are today in Latin America—will want to retract or relativise a single word of this moving homage. 'Greater love has no man than this, that a man lay down his life for his friends' (John 15:13).

Christian martyrs

The Christian who enters the revolutionary struggle does not set up his spirituality over against the Marxist as if it were a contest. He will simply live out his faith as loyally and confidently as he can, with the help of the Holy Spirit. It is not, therefore, my intention, to compare Christian and communist spirituality, but to indicate what seems to me basic for a Christian spirituality within the struggle for human liberation. Again, these are only very simple and initial lines—only real life will develop them.

The 'spiritual trinity' which the Christian tradition has picked up from Paul's thirteenth chapter of First Corinthians seems to me still the best characterisation of Christian spirituality: faith, hope and love, not as separate 'virtues' but as a plural and at the same time single reality, as the operation of the Holy Spirit in the Christian community. Again it has been Moltmann, in his beautiful meditation on hope, that has given us a profound articulation of this unity. Faith is the ground of hope while hope is the mobilising horizon of faith: 'Hope is nothing else than the expectation of those things which faith has believed to have been truly promised by God ... faith is the foundation upon which hope rests, hope nourishes and sustains faith'.[3] Love, on the other hand, gives faith a concrete human content in the direction of the fulfilment of hope. Faith is the power and hope is the perseverance of love: 'In its hope, love surveys the open possibilities of history. In love, hope brings all things into the light of the promise of God.'[4] This spirituality of faith, hope and love in their unity is particularly relevant in the conditions of revolutionary struggle. This, at least in three different but complementary directions:

It means utter availability for service. Salvation by grace, through faith, means that a man does not find his identity and reality any longer in himself but in Christ. He is not constituted as human being in isolation but in a free and generous relationship made available from outside himself. He has, therefore, no self-image to preserve, no face to save, no status to defend — his image, status, face have once for all been assured in Jesus Christ and 'nobody can take it away from him' because 'nothing can separate us from Christ's love'. A Christian is, therefore, totally available. In the beautiful words of John Wesley's covenant prayer, he can say:

> I am no longer my own, but Thine. Put me to what Thou wilt, rank me with whom Thou wilt; put me to doing, put me to suffering; let me be employed for Thee or laid aside for Thee; exalted for Thee or brought low for Thee; let me be full, let me be empty; let me have all things, let me have nothing; I freely and heartily yield all things to Thy pleasure and disposal.

It is in this total surrender that even one's own subjectivity, doubts, uncertainties and inconsistencies are overcome, not in the dissolution of the self, nor on the twilight of cynicism and indifference or in the proud objectivity of an infallible human cause but in the simple trust of faith. As Bonhoeffer looking at his own divided self under the trial of imprisonment, one can say: 'Whatever I am, Lord, you know it, I am thine.'

In the second place, availability means a commitment unto death. The hope of the resurrection has frequently been denounced — and not without justification — as paralysing, as an easy comfort that deters man from historical action. We have heard Bloch commenting on it as compromising the purity of self-sacrifice. But it seems to me that, at its best, it means something much deeper and more dynamic. In faith, the Christian has left his death behind him; to that extent he does not need to make an effort to ensure his own life. There is, therefore, an availability which cannot be limited by the threat that otherwise seems insuperable—death. A Christian can risk his life. Many have done it (not always for the best causes, to be sure!). Non-Christians have also done it, moved by a love which believers cannot but admire and for which they praise God. What matters here, nevertheless, is to become conscious of the freedom for self-giving available to those who know that 'death . . . cannot separate us from the love of Christ'. The strength of this argument cannot be proved in discourse but in the lives of Christians — the names of Martin Luther King or Camilo Torres immediately come to mind—who have really put their lives on the line so that others might have a better life.

Every process of social transformation, on the other hand, even those so-called non-violent, is costly. There are people and groups that suffer. It is clear—as we have argued before—that such sacrifices can only be requested with a consideration of the human and ethical factors and, most importantly, when it is done justly: for all. But, on the other side, Christians should show their availability by being ready to go beyond what is demanded, to pay in their own person—*payer de sa personne*, as the beautiful French sentence puts it—the cost of transformation. This means to pay out of their comfort, their status, their work, their own life. But there is more: the sacrifice demanded from those who cannot understand it, those who will only know pain, suffering, toil and death. It is difficult to see how a simple appeal to the welfare of future generations, or to the solidarity of the species, can adequately answer this question unless personal existence is totally dissolved into a collective 'social formation' which is therefore devoid of all human meaning.[5] There is no compensation for personal existence; it is not simply a *cost* which can be compensated by some *gain*. It seems to us that only a faith that transcends death can responsibly undertake the awful decision of indispensable but costly transformations. This is, to be sure, a very dangerous argument, and one which can be easily distorted. But it seems that it is a decisive ethical element, which has to be considered in any realistic understanding of a revolutionary situation.

These last words have already introduced the question of the suffering inherent in ethical action. For the Christian this is an inevitable and meaningful fact. Its roots go back to the very nature of Christian life and the relation to Jesus Christ. To be a believer means to participate in the movement of love which brought Jesus Christ to share our human life, emptying himself of his power and glory and assuming the fragility, the temptation and even the guilt of man, giving his own life even unto the death of the cross. What is here at stake is not a mere 'imitation' but a participation in the lot of solidary love, the only thing that can really create a possibility of new life for man. For this reason, the Apostle Paul does not hesitate in referring to his own suffering — physical as well as spiritual — as his participation in 'what still has to be fulfilled in the sufferings of Christ'. It is not that Christ left something undone, but that he opened for us a way of serving men in which the disciple enters now, paying the price or, as Jesus himself said, 'taking up his cross'.

Not every suffering has this character: it is that suffering which results from taking in love responsibility for others: 'nobody has a greater love than this, that he may give his life for his friends', or, as Paul comments, for those whom he loves, even though they may still consider themselves his enemies. It is the inevitable suffering that comes with service. Why? Because we live in a world which has turned its back to love, the world of injustice, the world which accepts the norms of the anti-Kingdom. Whoever undertakes (whether Christian or not) to introduce that which corresponds to true humanity, justice and peace, has final reality on his side, but the present structure of the world (for us, at present, very concretely as a capitalist order!) against him. The old world resents his presence and tries to eliminate him. Sometimes it succeeds — and then his solidarity with Christ is fulfilled: he 'witnesses . . . unto blood'.

We must try to understand carefully what is here in question. It is not the masochism which finds satisfaction in suffering or rejection. To be a disciple is, in Christian terms, to enlist in a conflict which is still raging, however much its outcome may be evident to faith. To share the lot of the Captain, to be found 'worthy of suffering for Christ and with him', to place body and soul side by side with him—and (with him) with those for whom he came—is the greatest joy of the soldier. To share in the victory, to participate in the triumphal procession, is not an isolated privilege that one 'buys' through suffering: it is part of that very same participation, of having become one—rather, having been made one—with the Lord. And victory and celebration are the triumph of love, the consummation of the Kingdom on which the hope of all—the victor and the defeated—hangs equally. The triumph of God is the welfare of men. For this the Christian will be glad to pay the price.

Be glad: in faith and hope, the final victory is already present. And therefore tragedy, suffering and death do not have the final word. The Brazilian theologian Rubem Alves has very acutely underlined 'the political significance of the Sabbath': it is the day that represents 'the politics of God', the fact that, beyond our toil and effort, our commitment and seriousness, our concern and responsibility, lies the certainty of God's own promise. We do not carry the burden of the whole world on our back, we carry only the burden of the day. We can rest! God himself can rest and simply enjoy the praise of creation because the 'goodness' of his work, however compromised in the struggle, cannot be undone. And we can rest—we can pray, and play, and love, and laugh—in the midst of toil. Therefore, there is nothing contradictory, but quite to the contrary, the deepest secret and ethos of Christian spirituality, in Paul's paradoxical exhortation: 'Rejoice in suffering!'

I cannot but feel that there is a deep and fundamental lack in Marxist philosophy at this point; an impossibility to make sense of the experience of joy, personal fulfilment, hope and love which many of the militants have so beautifully illustrated. The very life of Marx is full of a deep compassion, a sensitivity to friendship and joy, a love of beauty, which finds little place in his view of man as a mere 'determinate species-being'. I cannot refrain from quoting from a letter written in 1856 (the year in which he was deeply involved in working for *Das Kapital*) to his 'dearest darling' (his wife):

> But love—not of Feuerbachian man, not of Moleschott's metabolisms, not of the proletariat, but love of one's darling, namely you, *makes a man into a man again*. In fact there are many women in the world, and some of them are beautiful. But where can I find another face in which every trait, even every wrinkle brings back the greatest and sweetest memories of my life? Even my infinite sorrows, my irreplaceable losses I can read on your sweet countenance, and I kiss my sorrows away when I kiss your sweet face. 'Buried in your arms, awoken by your kisses'—that is, in your arms and by your kisses, and the Brahmins and Pythagoreans can keep their doctrine of reincarnation and Christianity its doctrine of resurrection.[6]

This is not merely the new 'social man' which a change in the mode of production can create (although a competitive and inhuman mode of production can deprive man, and does deprive many a man, of the possibility of experiencing and bringing to consciousness this love). This is a testimony of a humanity that roots deeper than the commitment to a human cause. How can this human experience—and many another that could be mentioned—be seen, and lived, not as a distraction from commitment, not as a substitute for responsibility, but in a unity and integrity in which it reinforces, gives depth and meaning to the struggle?

These last pages are not an attempt to extol Christian spirituality as an argument. A Christian knows that faith is not at the end of a syllogism. He will simply offer his witness, not so much in words but in his life. Or rather, in the words that participate in the texture of his life. Such witness is always an invitation, extended in hope and joy, to that kind of life which is for us present and permanent reality, the life in Christ. In the community of human struggle, Christian faith becomes an invitation under the conditions of responsible, joyful solidary militancy.

It is necessary, particularly where we have been dealing with the most 'spiritual' dimensions of Christian life to remind ourselves that we are still speaking about political and social engagement—we are still in the world of social struggle, economic considerations, political programme, revolutionary theory, perhaps jail and torture, in any case conflict. It is here that the Christian lives his witness. Perhaps some of us will not share the course of action, nor agree with the political and tactical decisions chosen by Néstor Paz, a young Bolivian Christian who joined the guerrillas and died of starvation in the jungle. But I can hardly think of a more appropriate expression of Christian spirituality than the last entry in his diary:

> You know, God, that I have tried by all means to be faithful to you . . . This is why I am here. I see love as the urgency to solve the problem of the other person, in whom you meet me. I left everything I had and came here. Today is perhaps my Thursday and this night my Friday. I lay everything I am in your hands with a trust that has no limits because I love you . . . because you are my Father. No death is useless if the life has been heavy with meaning, and I think this is true of us. Goodbye, Lord; until that Heaven of yours, that new world we desire so much!

NOTES

Chapter I   Communists and Theologians

1 *Fidel en Chile; textos completos de su diálogo con el pueblo* (Santiago de Chile, Editorial Quimantu, 1972), p. 92.

2 Juan Rosales, *Los cristianos, los marxistas y la revolución* (Buenos Aires, Ediciones Sílaba, 1970), p. 35. Italics as in the original.

3 Luis N. Rivera Pagain, 'Aportes del Marxismo' in *Pueblo oprimido, Señor de la historia* (ed. H. Assmann, Montevideo, Editorial Tierra Nueva, 1972), p. 249.

4 *Op. cit.*, p. 35.

5 Roger Garaudy in a postscript to the book by Giulio Girardi, *Marxisme et Christianisme* (Paris, Desclée de Brouwer, 1968), p. 303.

6 Julio de Santa Ana, 'Christian presence in a revolutionary society', in *World Mission and World Communism* (ed. G. Hoffmann and W. Wille, Edinburgh, The Saint Andrew Press, 1970), p. 63.

7 Lawrence Bright, O.P., 'Christian and Marxist', *What kind of revolution* (ed. J. Klugmann and P. Oestreicher, London, Panther Books, 1968), p. 125 f.

8 *Habla Fidel Castro sobre los cristianos revolutionarios* (ed. H. Assmann, Montevideo, Editorial Tierra Nueva, 1972), p. 108. My italics.

9 Ibid., Preface, p. 12.

10 I have tried to offer a more detailed account of the development of a revolutionary consciousness among Latin American Christians in the book *Doing Theology in a Revolutionary World* (Philadelphia, Fortress Press, 1975), chapters I–III. Cf. also an analysis of the process among some Protestant groups in 'Visión del cambio social y sus tareas desde las iglesias cristianas no-católicas' en *Fe cristiana y cambio social en América Latina* (Salamanca, Ediciones Sígueme, 1973), pp. 179–203.

11 *Father Camilo Torres; Revolutionary Writings* (ed. by Mauricio Zeitlin; New York, Harper and Row, 1972), pp. 217 ff. A more dramatic presentation is in the 'Message to Christians', *ibid.*, p. 314 ff.

12 Ibid., p. 231.

13 '*Una izquierda cristiana?*' (Lima, Perú, Centro de Estudios y Publicaciones, CEP, Apartado 6118, Lima, 1972), p. 29. For a summary history of the Chilean political parties, see George W. Grayson, J., *El Partido Demócrata Cristiano Chileno* (Buenos Aires, F. de Aguirre, 1968); Alejandro Silva Bascunán, *Una experiencia social cristiana* (Santiago de Chile, Editorial del Pacífico, 1949), Alberto Edwards Vives y Eduardo Frei Montalva, *Historia de los partidos políticos chilenos* (Santiago de Chile, Editorial del Pacífico, 1949). A summary in English in J.-P. Bernard, S. Cerqueira et al., *Guide to the Political Parties of South America* (Middlesex, England, Penguin Books, 1973), pp. 236–76.

14 The paragraph in question is found in K. Marx, F. Engels, *Werke* (Berlin, 1956 ff., 39 vols., hereafter cited as MEW), vol. 13/8 ff. In English it can be found in the *Selected Works*, identified hereafter as MESW (Moscow, 1935), I/362 ff.

15 Ignacio Sotelo, 'Der historische Ort des Marxismus in Lateinamerika' in *Marxismusstudien* (ed. by U. Duchrow, Tübingen, J. C. B. Mohr, 1969), Sechste Folge, pp. 65–114.

16 Ernesto Guevara, *Diario del Ché en Bolivia* (Lima, Perú, Francisco Moncloa editores S. A., s/d). See particularly entries for 10/2 and 17/3, the monthly summaries, the entry of 19/6.

17 *Orientaciones y Conclusiones de la Semana Internacional de Catéquesis*, Com. 6, Nr. 3.

18 'El Cristianismo, su plusvalía ideológica y el costo social de la revolución socialista', in *Cuadernos de la Realidad Nacional* (Santiago de Chile), No. 12, April 1972, pp. 154–79.

19 Cf. the articles by Carlos Ossa, Pablo Richard, Hugo Assmann in the journal *Cuadernos de la Realidad Nacional*, No. 19.

20 Although in a different form, Christianity plays also a paralysing role among the middle sectors of society which, however secularised in terms of style of living, keep a great sensitivity for whatever is presented as 'Christian values' or 'our Christian tradition'. There is a constant manipulation of these attitudes by the right, appealing to such notions as 'peace', or 'freedom', or 'order' over against the picture of an anarchic, oppressive and violent revolution. It is precisely in these areas of society where the unblocking effect of a

new 'reading' of the Christian faith which impels social change has made its first impact. The possibility that this will also happen among the masses is still in a very embryonic stage at the practical level; it is a hypothesis based on certain facts but that has yet to be tried in practice.

21 See note 19.

22 Hugo Assmann, in the 'Preface' to *Habla Fidel Castro sobre los cristianos revolucionarios* (cf. note 8), p. 18.

23 Quoted in the 'Final Document' of the Santiago meeting of *Cristianos por el Socialismo* (Santiago de Chile, Editorial Mundo Nuevo, 1972), p. 302.

24 Cf. particularly Lenin's writing 'On Religion'.

Chapter II   Blessed are the Doers

1 In the selection and interpretation of this Biblical material I recognise my indebtedness to the excellent work of the Mexican Biblical scholar José Porfirio Miranda, whose two books: *Marx y la Biblia* (México, edición del autor, 1970) y *El Ser y el Mesías* (Salamanca, Ediciones Sígueme, 1973) are an example of the serious and creative exegetical and hermeneutical study being done today in Latin America.

2 G. Johannes Botterweck, '*Gott erkennen*' (Bonn, Peter Hanstein Verlag, 1951), p. 45.

3 The force of many of these texts has been concealed by a subjectivistic and sentimental interpretation of '*hesed*', variously translated as 'mercy', 'love', 'faithfulness', etc. In the Bible itself, such misinterpretation is prevented by the frequent synonymous parallelism (of *endiadis*) with justice (*sedaqah*) or right (*mishpat*). For instance, Jer. 9:23; Isa. 16:5; Mic. 6:8; Hos. 2:19; 6:6; 10:12; 12:6; Zech. 7:9; Ps. 25:10; 33:5; 36:6; 40:11; 85:11; 88:12; 89:15; 98:2; 103:17; 119: 62 ff. The rabbinical tradition, keeping a close relationship between '*hesed*' and the Law, has run the opposite danger of a legalistic and restrictive interpretation, but has preserved the objective and social content of the original.

4 H. W. Wolff, 'Dodekapropheton', in *Biblischer Kommentar* (Neukirchener Verlag, 1965), Vol. I, p. 84.

5 Op. cit., p. 97.

6 *El Ser y el Mesías*, esp. chapters 4–6.

7 For a further study of the meaning of the expression 'good works', compare the following texts: Isa. 58:6–7; 1 Tim. 5:10, 25; 6:18;

2 Tim. 2:21; 3:17; Eph. 2:10; Col. 1:10; 2 Thess. 2:17; Matt.
5:16; Mark 3:4; Acts 10:38; Titus 1:16; 2:14; 3:1; 8, 14; 2 Cor.
9:8; Rom. 13:3; Mic. 6:8.

8 Ibid., p. 79.

9 One must admit that this characterisation is not altogether just to
existentialism, which is precisely an attempt to overcome this
'objectifying' relation to a metaphysical essence. But, to the extent
that it substitutes a formal analysis of the existential moment of
decision or encounter for the content-filled interpolation of the
Word, it has the same consequence of blurring the specific identity
of the God of the Bible.

Chapter III The Opiate of the People

1 Marx/Engels *Gesamtausgabe* (Frankfurt, Verlagsgesellschaft
M.B.H., 1927 ff.). Hereafter quoted as MEGA; I, 1, 1, p. 606. In
English in the selection *Marx and Engels on Religion* (New York,
Schocken Books, 1967; reprint from the Moscow edition of the
Foreign Language Publishing House, 1957), p. 41.

2 MEW, vol. 27/412.

3 'Debates on the Freedom of the Press'. in *Early Texts* (ed.
McLellan; Oxford, Oxford University Press, 1971), p. 35. MEW,
vol. I/35.

4 Ibid., loc. cit.

5 MEGA, I, 1, 1, p. 246: *Marx and Engels on Religion* p. 35.

6 Marx had already written in 1842: 'It is not religion which creates
man . . . but man who creates religion', MEGA I, 1, 1, p. 434.

7 Ibid., p. 435.

8 'On the Jewish Question', MEGA, I, 1, 1, p. 590, cf. p. 587.

9 MEGA I, 1, 1, p. 497.

10 Ibid., MEGA, I, 1, 1, p. 598.

11 'Contribution to the Critique of Hegel's Philosophy of Right',
MEGA, I, 1, 1, p. 608; *Marx and Engels on Religion*, p. 42.

12 'On the Jewish Question', MEGA I, 1, 1, p. 590.

13 Ibid., loc. cit.

14 Ibid., MEGA, I, 1, 1, p. 603. There is no place here to discuss the
vexed question of the exact status and meaning of Marx's use of
the concept of alienation, drawn from the philosophical tradition,
and particularly from Hegel. While I would concur with those
who hold that it is present throughout Marx's whole work, it is
also true that the meaning changes and that this change moves

towards greater precision in the economic writings (as the use of the word itself becomes scarcer).

15 *Das Kapital*, Book I, ch. 1, par. 4. MEW, Vol. 23, p. 86.

16 Ibid., see the whole section on par. 3 and 4.

17 'Letter against Kriege', in MEGA I, 6, p. 1–21.

18 'Class struggles in France', MEW. Vol. 7, p. 56.

19 MEGA, I, 1, 1, p. 607.

20 'Socialism and Religion', a speech of Dec. 1905, in V. I. Lenin, *Collected Works* (Moscow, Foreign Language Publishing House, 1962), Vol. 10, p. 83. Lenin has discussed the relation of the communist-Marxist revolution to religion in a number of articles which have had a great influence in the attitude of the communist parties. In general, one could say that: (1) he has repeated the Marxist view of religion as an imaginary sublimation of man's real economic alienation; (2) he has denounced even more strongly than Marx and Engels the ideological use of religion against the people; (3) in the struggle against the social-democratic (Second International) and some religious communists in Russia, he rejected all compromise with religious tendencies; (4) he considered the struggle against religious fantasy and superstition a fundamental task of the Communist Party; (5) he defended a total secularisation of the state (including education, culture, etc.), but insisted on maintaining freedom for the private exercise of religion; (6) he rejected any idea of an anti-religious crusade, or of considering the anti-religious struggle a top priority: if religion is a reflex of a more fundamental alienation, then it can only be eradicated through the elimination of this economic alienation.

21 Jean Roux, *Précis historique et théorique du Marxisme-Léninisme* (Paris, Robert Laffont, 1969), pp. 303, 304, 307, 309–12.

22 Lenin, op. cit.

23 The Ilitchev Report, published by the bi-monthly *Kommunist* (1964, No. 1, Jan. 17, 1964). We quote from the Spanish version in *Informaciones Católicas Internacionales* (No. 211, March 7, 1964), pp. 15–31.

24 I quote from the Italian version, published together with the reports of the XXII Congress in *Rapporti e discorso conclusivo al XXII Congresso del PCUS* (Roma, Editori Riuniti, 1962), p. 206.

25 Ibid., p. 126.

26 *Tesi del X Congresso* (Roma, Editori Riuntii, 1963), cap. I, par. 8, p. 666.

27 P. Togliatti in a speech at Bergamo on March 20, 1963.

28 Lucio Lombardo Radice, 'Un marxista ante hechos nuevos del pensamiento y de la conciencia religiosa', in *El diálogo de la época; cristianos y marxistas* (Spanish translation; Buenos Aires, Editorial Platina, 1965), pp. 75–96.

29 Some of the best examples will be found in the work of Ernst Bloch, *Atheismus in Christentum* and of V. Gardavsky, *Gott is nicht ganz tot* (ET, *God is not yet dead*, Pelican 1973).

30 Giulio Girardi, *Marxisme et Christianisme* (Paris, Desclée, 1968), pp. 153–5; English translation *Marxism and Christianity* (New York, The Macmillan Co., 1968), pp. 134–7.

31 Ibid., pp. 303 ff. (The English Translation does not include Garaudy's Postface). We quote here from 'Significación humana del socialismo', in *La reconquista de la esperanza* (Caracas, Monte Avila Editores, 1972) p. 95 ff.

32 Henry Desroches, *Socialismes et sociologie religieuse* (Paris, Editions Cujas, 1965), p. 407 ff. A valuable bibliographical note is included by Desroches (Ibid., n. 3).

Chapter IV   The Biblical Criticism of Religion

1 Quoted by H. H. Schrey, 'Die Kirche und die soziale Frage', in *Theologische Rundschau*, 1953; p. 26 ff.

2 K. Marx, 'The Communism of the paper Rheinische Beobachter' (oroginally published in September 1847), in *Marx and Engels on Religion*, p. 83.

3 Helmut Gollwitzer, *Athéisme marxiste et foi chrétienne* (Paris, Casterman, 1965). There is a German original and also an English translation.

4 Giulio Girardi, 'Christianity and Marxism', *LADOC Papers*, III, 18b., January 1973, p. 10.

5 Walter Dirks, 'Marxismus in christlicher Sicht', in *Frankfurter Hefte*, February 1947, p. 141 ff., quoted by Gollwitzer, op. cit., p. 112.

6 Ibid., loc. cit.

7 In the Introduction to 'Contribution to the Critique of Hegel's Philosophy of Right'; *Marx and Engels on Religion*, p. 51.

8 Engels in 'Ludwig Feuerbach and the outcome of German Philosophy', MEW, Vol. 21, p. 303, and in a letter to Mehring on July 14, 1893, MEW, vol. 39, p. 96 ff.

9 Ludovico Silva, *Teoría y práctica de la ideología* (Mexico, Editorial Nuestro Tiempo, 1971), p. 17 ff., n. 5.

10 'The economic-philosophical Manuscripts' (1844), MEGA I, 1, 1, 3, pp. 83, 84, 90.
11 MEGA I, 1, 1, p. 10; *Marx and Engels on Religion*, p. 15.
12 Quoted by Jan M. Lochman, *Christus oder Prometheus?* (Hamburg, Furch Verlag, 1972), p. 51.
13 'Christianity and Marxism', op. cit., p. 8. Emphasis added.
14 MEGA I, 1, 1, p. 583.

Chapter V   The Exaltation and the Abolition of Man

1 W. A. Visser 't Hooft, 'The Christian in World Affairs', in *The Student World* (Vol. XVI, 2; Second Quarter 1948), p. 112. Cf. his article in *Christianity and Crisis*, Vol. IX, No. 13, July 1949, pp. 98–103.
2 M. Merleau Ponty, *Humanisme et Terreur* (Paris, 1947), p. 13.
3 Louis Althusser, 'Marxismo y Humanismo', in *Polémica sobre marxismo y humanismo* (México, Editorial Siglo Veintiuno, 1972), p. 6 ff.
4 'Contribution to the Critique of Hegel's Philosophy of Right', MEGA, I, 1, 1, p. 614; *Marx and Engels on Religion*, p. 50.
5 Op. cit., p. 20.
6 Ernesto Guevara, *Obras Completas* (Buenos Aires, Editorial del Plata, 1967), Vol. II, pp. 19, 24. Marx himself had once said: 'the proletariat, that will not suffer to be treated like rabble, values its courage, its self-respect, its pride and its independence more than its bread', MEW, 4, p. 200.
7 'The poverty of philosophy', MEGA, I, 1, 6, p. 179; *Works* (Moscow edition), p. 122. I have taken the quotation from a relatively early text of 'the mature Marx' for two reasons: directed against Proudhon, it emphasises the new elements over against Marx's own previous position; in a simple form it gives account of the new theory—Marx himself suggested reading it as an introduction to *Das Kapital*.
8 Ibid., p. 191; ET, p. 140.
9 Ibid., p. 228; ET, p. 196.
10 There is an introduction to the thought of some of these men, although in a rather superficial and flippant manner, in the book of McInnes, *The Western Marxists* (London, Alcove Press, 1972).
11 Op. cit., p. 15.
12 Ibid., p. 16.
13 Ibid., p. 15. In his article 'L'object du Capital', in *Lire Le Capital*

(Vol. II, p. 73), he recognises that 'a-humanism' would be a more accurate expression, but justifies his use of the stronger word in the need to counter the humanist ideologies that, in his view, 'have not ceased to threaten Marxism for the last forty years'.

14 Op. cit., p. 33.

15 Cf., among other, Lucien Sève, *Marxisme et théorie de la personalité* (Paris, Editions Sociales, 1974) and Helmut Fleischer, *Marxismus und Geschichte* (Frankfurt a.M., Suhrkamp Verlag, 1972).

Chapter VI   Towards an Ethical Evaluation of Marxism

1 'The poverty of Philosophy', MEGA, I, 1, 6, p. 227; ET p. 196.

2 Maximilien Rubel, *Pages de Karl Marx pour une éthique socialiste* (Paris, Editions Payot, 1970; 2 vols.). Rubel argues that in its very essence Marx's thought is an ethical message: the historical mission of the proletariat and the self-emancipation of the worker in order to further the realisation of the total man and of a society free from alienation. Marx, according to Rubel, related this ethos to the notion of 'historical necessity' through his scientific analysis of the capitalist society, thus forcing man to decide in relation to an alternative: either the proletariat assumes its historical mission and mankind moves towards a socialist society, or the contradictions of the system lead to chaos and destruction. This significant hypothesis for the interpretation of Marx is substantiated in a long introduction and a careful and balanced anthology of Marx's most significant work. Concerning the Marxist concept of solidarity, it will be useful to see the first part of Girardi's book, already quoted (cf. pp. 159–96; ET, pp. 140–72).

3 Lenin, Speech of October 2, 1920, in *Obras escogidas* (Moscow, n.d.), p. 641. My italics.

4 I am thinking particularly of the work of the Argentine historian and philosopher Enrique Dussel, who has developed this theme extensively in a critical analysis of European philosophy. Cf., his book *Para una ética de la liberación latinoamericana* (Buenos Aires, Siglo Veintiuno editores, 1973, 2 vols.), to which I am indebted for this point.

5 In order to avoid a mere formalisation of this idea, it would be important to introduce here the concrete perspective in which this presence of 'the other' is portrayed in the Bible: it is the poor, the foreigner, the unprotected, the man who has fallen in the hands of the robbers! God himself reveals his identity by being 'the God of

the poor', the God whose name cannot be man's possession but who offers to the oppressed and name-less the power to become a people, to have a name.

Chapter VII God in Heaven and God in History

1 Quoted by David McLellan, *Karl Marx: his life and thought* (London, Macmillan, 1973), p. 28.

2 It is worth noting, in passing, that when the Bible speaks of God's relationship with 'the nations', 'the gentiles', it models this relationship after the same pattern of concrete, historical and responsible relations. The 'oracles to the nations' in Amos 1 and 2 and the discussion of the moral responsibility of the gentiles in Romans 1 presuppose a covenantal relationship in which the law of human solidarity, of justice and reverence is included, and which is based in God's own creative and providential initiative and self-manifestation (cf. Amos 9:7, Acts 17:24 ff., Rom. 1:19 ff.).

3 The books by the European Marxists Gardavsky and Bloch, which we have mentioned before (ch. III, n. 29) explore this 'promethean' motif in Scriptures, and specifically in Christology. But they do it in a reductionist way because they still remain captive of the disjunctive God/man. Thus, particularly Bloch is forced to introduce a dichotomy between a promethean Christ (in the model of 'the serpent' which certain early Christian heresies already had used) and the Father, a dichotomy which runs counter to the basic Biblical witness. For a profound and illuminating discussion of these works see the book of Lochman already mentioned (ch. IV, n. 12).

4 This concrete, material nature of the 'spiritual' acts of faith, repentance, conversion, shows again how far is the Bible from all idealistic, individualistic or subjectivistic interpretations. It is extremely necessary and urgent to recover and re-think this dimension with regards to Christian evangelisation, because a call to faith articulated in an idealistic philosophy and psychology transforms evangelisation into alienating proselytism: a call to an abstract Christ who resembles more the *soter* of mystery religions than the Messiah announced by the prophets. Even when such evangelisation tries afterwards to 'supplement' such a formal conversion through 'moral obligation', the fatal dichotomy has already been consummated. Love becomes a 'second', subsidiary thing and the action of love is relegated to the area of 'consequences' of salvation and not, as in the Bible, the 'stuff', of the

covenant. The gratuitous character of salvation is wrongly under-stood as lack of historical content, as human emptiness and there-fore the Gospel brings no challenge. In order to overcome this deadly misunderstanding, theology needs, on the one hand, to repossess the Biblical witness in its concrete and material historicity and, on the other hand, it has to revise the psychology on which it operates and understand the way in which human personality is really constituted. The 'new man in Christ' is not an abstraction but the emergence of a new 'personhood' constituted in love and solidarity. And personality is created within the network and in the praxis of social and material relationships. Faith is not in the Bible something which takes place 'between Christ and the soul', but a public affair, involving man in his historicity, his relationships and his whole productive forces.

5 This argument is developed particularly in his book *The Art of Loving* (New York, Harper and Brothers, 1956).

6 While critical of Fromm's construction of Marxist humanism, an interpreter who clings to the more 'materialist' interpretation of Marx like the German Fleischer, nevertheless makes a similar point contrasting the kind of human being which belongs to capitalism and socialism: 'To be recognised by other men is a primary and universal need, but the proportions of mutual recognition can be very varied. The limit is *the equal recognition of fuller mutuality* (which is, in Marxism, the *anthropological norm* for communist society) . . .', op. cit., p. 56, cf. p. 72 ff.

Chapter VIII   The Promise and the Limits of the Alliance

1 Lawrence Bright, O.P., 'Christian and Marxist' in J. Klugmann and P. Oestreicher, (eds.), *What kind of Revolution?; A Christian-Communist Dialogue* (London, Panther Books, 1968), pp. 124–6.

2 I have tried to discuss this question at greater length in the book *Doing Theology in a Revolutionary Situation* (Philadelphia, Fortress Press, 1975), cap. VI.

3 Again, it has been in Italian communism where the possibility of a pluralism in philosophical and religious viewpoint and unity in revolutionary theory and practice has been more deeply explored. In this respect Lucio Lombardo Radice has offered a very interest-ing thesis. He recognises that 'historical materialism' as a science of history (which he believes indispensable to revolutionary theory) was born of 'dialectical materialism' as a philosophy.

But such a science of history, he claims, like other scientific discoveries bound in their origin to philosophical viewpoints, is not necessarily dependent on the acceptance of the originating philosophy. 'This discovery', he says referring to the Marxist interpretation of history, 'once reached, has become a *lay* truth, which validates itself for men who profess the more diverse philosophies, as an understanding and description of a real process, as *knowledge* that has inherent validity, a life of its own which is independent of the philosophical hypothesis which stimulated its discovery', 'Sí, para suerte nuestra', in *Cuadernos de Pasado y Presente*, No. 8, July 1969, p. 91 (the original was published in the Italian Journal *Rinascita*, Nos. 11, 13 and 14 (1968/1969).

4 Gustavo Gutiérrez, *A Theology of Liberation* (New York, Orbis Books, 1973), Par. 11, III, 'Faith, utopia and political action'.

5 Of course, not all utopian thinking has this positive character; it can also be alienating, distracting people from a serious concern for reality, and it can be destructive when it mobilises in the service of inhuman or sectarian visions of man and society.

6 *Theology of Hope* (New York, Harper and Row, 1967), p. 16.

7 M. Rubel, op. cit., Vol. I, pp. 37–42.

8 MEW, II, p. 148.

9 MEGA, vol, 20, pp. 168–69, 262–63.

Chapter IX   Red Heroes and Christian Martyrs

1 Eric Hoffer, *The True Believer* (New York, Harper and Row, 1951) p. 151. This is a rather cynical book, in which commitment is treated as a perverse flight from the self. But it is useful in pointing out some of the psycho-social mechanisms that operate in it, and the danger inherent in any thorough-going devotion to a cause. Its basic fallacy, though, is to treat commitment as a purely formal thing, without realising that the nature of the devotion is shaped by its object.

2 Ernst Bloch, *Das Prinzip Hoffnung* (Frankfurt, Suhrkamp Verlag, 1959), Vol. III, p. 1378 ff.

3 Op. cit., p. 20.

4 Ibid., p. 32.

5 Marx's own thinking is particularly poor in relation to the question of 'death'. In the 'Paris Manuscripts' he comments that 'death appears as the harsh victory of the species over the particular individual and seems to contradict their unity; but the particular

individual is only a determinate species-being and thus mortal' (*Early Texts*, p. 151; MEGA I, 1, 3, p. 117). There is little here to meet the reality of death as the human race has experienced it since the dawn of history. Girardi (op. cit., pp. 96–98, ET., pp. 79–82) has treated this question, coming to the conclusion that the problem has no possible answer within Marxism. When Garaudy answers him (Ibid., pp. 313 f.), he quotes the aforementioned paragraph of Marx and speaks of the 'pedagogical' value of death, as a teacher of generosity and self-forgetfulness. Again, this simply is evasive. In my own interpretation, the courage in front of death and suffering which so many Marxists have shown is much more related to the love that motivates their participation in the struggle that in any 'self-forgetfulness' which the certainty of annihilation or the abstract concept of 'species' could generate.

6 MEW, vol. XXIX, p. 532. Quoted by McLellan, op. cit., p. 274.

INDICES

I. Biblical References

2. Names and Subjects